MW00635572

OUTREACH
IN THE
TORAH

MOSAICA PRESS

OUTREACH IN THE TORAH

WEEKLY INSPIRATION and EXAMPLES of the MITZVAH of REACHING OUT

RABBI DOVID S. ASHER

ISBN: 978-1-952370-67-0

Published by Mosaica Press, Inc.
www.mosaicapress.com
info@mosaicapress.com

Rabbi Dovid Asher, rabbi of Knesseth Beth Israel of Richmond Virginia, has authored a work on the weekly parashah that accentuates the role of outreach, empathy, altruism, and unity in kelal yisrael's development, and that vigorously and passionately advocates the urgent need to promote this emphasis in our time. Rabbi Asher invokes principles like arevut (every Jew is a guarantor for the spiritual destiny of his fellow), kidush Hashem, and ahavat Hashem to reinforce his perspective and his analysis of the parshiyot. He elaborates not only on the obligation, but also the spiritual benefits of sharing torah study and the commitment to torah values and norms with others. Avraham avinu, the father of the nation and paradigm of outreach, sets the tone and typifies this aspiration. He is depicted as "Avraham ohavi" (Isaiah 41-Hashem's beloved) because his "kiruv" (ve-hanefesh asher asu be-haron) overflowed from his love and devotion to Hashem (see the author's devar torah for parshat Lekh Lekha, and also Rambam's Sefer ha-Mizvot, aseh no. 3).

Rabbi Asher, a long-time and cherished talmid, has exemplified this very emphasis and approach in his rabbanut in Richmond Va., where he has already made an indelible impression. I am proud of his personal and communal achievements, and especially admire his sincerity and his ability to empower others in their commitment and growth as ovdei Hashem and benei Torah. The publication of this sefer, which embodies his own convictions and priorities, is a significant accomplishment and one which foreshadows continued growth and impact. May he and his wonderful family continue their successful efforts in harbazat ha-torah, and in ahavat and kidush Hashem- להגדיל תורה ולהאדירה.

Be-birkat ha-torah,

Rav Michael Rosensweig
Rosh Yeshiva, Rosh Kollel
Yeshivat Rabbenu Yitzhak Elhanan
Yeshiva University

דוד קאהן

ביהמ"ד גבול יעבץ
ברוקלין, נוא יארק

מכתב ברכה

בס"ד

קראתי הקטעים מהספר על התורה מהרב
דוד אשר שליט"א. הנה ידועים דברי אחד מגדולי
בעלי מוסר שפי' ראה לי"ט שכותב הרא"ש ע"ד מהלכה
שכותב ומביא ראיה שהי' ראוי לו" מע"ד עליו הרא"ש
כמה שידע כל התורה כולה משא"כ ראיה אחת מהתורה.
מכיון שהמחבר עיקר עסקו הוא במה שהגלו מהרב
רבותינו ומשפיע עליהם יכול להרגיש מה דברי תורה
שלו שנאמרים בטוב טעם ודעת והדרגשה עמוקה להשפיע
טוב. והנני מברכו שימשיך בדרכיו להשפיע על עדתו
בהצלחה רבה.

הכותב לכבוד המשפיעים
על הציבור

דוד קאהן
כ"ט למטמונים תשפ"א

23 Iyar 5781

It has been an enormous pleasure watching Rav Dovid Asher grow over the years as a Talmid Chacham and as a beacon of light for the people of Israel. What a *zechus* I consider it – an honor and a privilege - to have contributed a small measure towards his growth as my *Talmid*. In so many capacities he has impacted on the people around him to inspire them to ascend the ladder of spiritual growth. He has had a profound impact upon his congregants in his wonderful community in Richmond , Virginia and on many others outside of his *Kehilla* as well.

Now Rav Dovid has taken upon himself an ambitious project, to reveal the Torah's insights into *Kiruv* in each and every *Parsha* in the Torah. This *Sefer* will no doubt enlighten those who are at the forefront of Jewish leadership but will be inspiring as well for all Jews everywhere. We wish him great success in all of his endeavors.

Azarya Berzon
Rav Kehilla and Rosh Kollel
Emek Learning Center
Yerushalayim

הרב נפתלי יהודה הלוי הורוויץ
בן הרה"צ לוי יצחק זצוק"ל - דער באסטאנער רבי
Grand Rabbi Naftali Y. Horowitz

ב"ה

יום ד' לסדר 'אש"ר רוח בו', כ' תמוז תשפ"א

למעלת כבוד ידידי החשוב והנעלה, מוציא יקר מזולל, אוהב את הבריות ומקרבן לתורה, הרה"ג רבי **דוד אשר** שליט"א, האיש על העדה בק"ק כנסת בית ישראל ריטשמאנד

שמחתי לשמוע כי הינך עומד להוציא לאור ספר חידושים נפלאים על התורה, דברים מתוקים מדבש ונופת צופים מעומק הגיונך הזך ומכפי נסיונך הגדול בקירוב רחוקים לכנפי השכינה, ואכן תורת ה' תמימה משיבת נפש – להשיב נפשות בני ישראל ולקרב לבבותיהם לאביהם שבשמים, ואין ערוך לפעליך הכבירים, וכאותם הדברים אשר כתב בעל החובות הלבבות (שער אהבת ה' פרק ו) 'וראוי לך אחי לדעת, כי זכיות המאמין אפילו אם יהיה מגיע אל התכלית הרחוקה בתקון נפשו לאלוקים ית', ואילו היה קרוב למלאכים במדותם הטובות ומנהגיהם המשובחים והשתדלותם בעבודת הבורא ואהבתם הזכה בו, אינם כזכיות מי שמורה בני אדם אל הדרך הטובה ומישר הרשעים אל עבודת הבורא שזכיותיו נכפלות בעבור זכיותם בכל הימים ובכל הזמנים'.

והנני בברכה נאמנה כי חפץ ה' בידך יצלח, ויהי דו"ד משכיל בכל דרכיו וה' עמו, ויפוצו מעיינותיך חוצה להשיב לב בנים לאבינו אב הרחמן, מתוך בריות גופא ונהורא מעליא לאורך ימים ושנים, דשנים ורעננים.

נפתלי יהודה הלוי הורוויץ
בן רבי לוי[illegible]

1710 BEACON STREET BROOKLINE MASSACHUSETTS 02445-2124 FAX: (617) 739-0163 PHONE: (617) 734-5100 EMAIL: rofeh@rofehint.org

BETH DIN ZEDEK
BETH DIN ZEDEK ECCLESIASTICAL JUDICATURE OF THE
CHICAGO RABBINICAL COUNCIL

2701 W. Howard Street * Chicago, Illinois 60645-1303
773-465-3900 FAX: 773-465-6632
email: info@crcweb.org

בית דין צדק דק"ק שיקגו והגליל
דמועצת הרבנים דשיקגו

בס"ד

הרב ישראל מאיר קרנו זצ"ל, ראב"ד מלפנים
RABBI ISRAEL M. KARNO, *of blessed memory*
Av Beth Din Emeritus

הרב חיים דוד רגנשברג זצ"ל, מייסד הבד"ץ
RABBI C. DAVID REGENSBERG, *of blessed memory*

הרב גדלי' דוב שווארץ, ראב"ד
RABBI GEDALIA DOV SCHWARTZ
Rosh Beth Din

הרב יונה ריס, אב"ד
RABBI YONA REISS
Av Beth Din

הרב אברהם מרדכי אברמסן
RABBI ALAN M. ABRAMSON
Menahel

כ"ג סיון תשע"ג

I have had the privilege of knowing Rabbi David Asher שליט"א for many years, including when he was a talmid at Yeshiva University and RIETS, and in his current capacity as the Rabbi of Keneseth Beth Israel in Richmond, Virginia. Rabbi Asher's most palpable quality is his יראת שמים, his all-encompassing reverence for the Almighty, and desire to spread His name and Torah to all those around him. The Gemora (יומא פו.) derives from the words in the Torah ואהבת את ה' אלקיך (דברים ו:ה) that שיהא שם שמים מתאהב על ידך – the name of Heaven should be made beloved by your actions. This book, which was written for the explicit purpose of imbuing the world with a sense of כבוד שמים – honor for the Almighty, constitutes a fulfillment of this imperative.

בברכת התורה ולמועדים,

יונה ריס

בס"ד

ישיבת רבנו יצחק אלחנן
Rabbi Isaac Elchanan Theological Seminary
An Affiliate of Yeshiva University

Rabbi Dovid Asher has been a student of mine in Yeshivas Rabbenu Yitzchak Elchanan and now serves as the Rabbi in Keneseth Beth Israel of Richmond, Virginia. This young Rabbi is revered for both his Torah scholarship and his interpersonal relationships.

Rabbi Asher has recently compiled his essays regarding -Kiruv-, connecting each parsha to this important mission. The notion of connecting Kiruv to the whole Torah echoes the words of the Talmud Sukkah (49b) that Torah which is taught to others is called Toras Chesed - a Torah of Kindness. Kiruv is the vehicle of this chesed and hence the entire Torah expresses this idea.

Rabbi Baruch Simon
Rosh Yeshiva Yeshivas Rabbenu Yitzchak Elchanan

RABBI BARUCH SIMON
O: 212.568.7300 F: 212.568.7400 www.yu.edu/riets
526 West 187th Street, Muss Hall, Room 111, New York, NY 10033-3201

Rav Yedidya Berzon
Rosh Mosdot Mevaseret

Rav Shimon Isaacson
Rosh Yeshiva

8 Sivan, 5781

Shalom U'vracha:

It is my honor to write a haskama for the new Sefer, "Outreach in the Torah," written by my dear talmid, HaRav Dovid Asher, shlit"a. It is well-known and well-documented how so many of our Jewish brethren find themselves estranged from Torah and Mitzva observance. They are distant not because of overt and reasoned choices that they made, but simply out of lack of connection or points of contact with authentic Judaism and sincere Torah observant Jews. If they had meaningful points of connection, no doubt the beauty of Judaism would resonate.

I want to share a brief story. When I was in law school, a visiting professor offered a shiur on legal sugyot in Masechet Sanhedrin. The shiur was open to anyone and twelve law students attended the optional opening lecture. I noticed two students that clearly weren't expecting or ready for an advanced Talmud class in arcane topics in gemara. The two were lost minutes into the shiur. After the class, I approached these two students, and noting that they didn't really follow the complex gemara shiur, I asked them if they would be interested in learning Sefer Bereishit with me. Happily, they said yes. After a few sessions, one of the two dropped out of this chevruta, but the other continued learning. Gradually, through the help of many he became religious and his children now learn in the finest of Yeshivot. I take no credit for any of his growth. All I take credit for is seizing a moment of potential connectivity with a fellow Jew who was clearly searching for more.

We live in a generation where there are so many potential points of contacts with those who might be searching for more spirituality and connectivity. So many opportunities are present, but all too often, they go untapped. That is why this Sefer is of such significance. No one needs to be told of the importance of Kiruv. That is obvious to all. But all too often, we get busy with the hustle and bustle of life, and we lose focus of the many opportunities to connect. Whether it be the workplace, the park, the bus stop, or the ballfield – there are so many points of contact. This Sefer is designed to help us stay focused and inspired by the many opportunities that present themselves.

Rav Dovid Asher is someone I am privileged to call a talmid. He has embarked on a masterful career as a Rav of a Shul and as a warm, engaging and humble community leader. He has been at the forefront of outreach for over twenty years, and he has made it a life mission to help others see the beauty of authentic Judaism. This Sefer is a work that draws lessons and inspiration for Kiruv from every parsha in the Torah. It is designed to help the reader maintain focus on one of the most important chasadim available to us. The reader will be uplifted by the timeless messages in the Sefer, and will hopefully be inspired to bring authentic Torah ideas and values to those seeking more.

We bless Rav Asher with much continued success in bringing Hashem's children close, and helping all Jews appreciate the unique mitzva of Outreach.

Rav Shimon Isaacson
Rosh Yeshiva,
Yeshivat Shaa'rei Mevaseret Tzion

50 Rechov HaOren PO Box 85899 Mevaseret Zion 90805
Tel: 972-2-533-9100 • Fax: 972-2-533-9101 • US line (Israel and US office hours): 212-444-1663
האורן 50, מבשרת ציון 90805
www.mevaseret.org • office@ysmz.org.il

R. Akiva David Kolchin
Rosh Kollel

Kollel Rischa D'Oraisa
41 Meshech Chochma
Kiryas Sefer (Modiin Illit)

When Rabbi Dovid Asher asked me to preview his manuscript, I was expecting to find a collection of enjoyable essays which would make pleasant reading. However, that is not what I found.

Instead I found a challenging sefer. This is a sefer which challenged me to ask myself meaningful questions about my life. Am I doing what I should be doing for the betterment of the Jewish people as a whole? Are my spiritual aspirations individual, or do I meaningfully aspire for our collective advancement in our relationship with the Almighty? Does it truly pain me when a secular Jew I've never met intermarries? Can my personal love of the Almighty be complete if it doesn't bring me to actively try to restore to Him His children who have drifted from Him and His Torah?

Rabbi Asher raises a question in his introduction - Who are we to assume that the makarev is closer to the Almighty than the person that he is being mekarev? The answer, which I understood from the sefer, is that kiruv is aimed at bringing the Jewish people as a whole closer to the Almighty. There is no question that this is accomplished by learning Torah and keeping the Mitzvos. Viewing kiruv in such a light makes the question irrelevant.

I thank Rabbi Asher for challenging me, and inspiring me.

R. Akiva David Kolchin
Rosh Kollel, Kollel Rischa D'Oraisa

TABLE OF CONTENTS

SEFER BEREISHIS

SEFER SHEMOS

SEFER VAYIKRA

SEFER BAMIDBAR

SEFER DEVARIM

FOREWORD

by Rabbi Steven Burg, CEO, Aish HaTorah

Even though the Almighty created the world, it did not take long for mankind to stray from His pathway. The immediate question became how to recalibrate humanity's direction in line with G-d. A hero arose who would start a movement to be a light unto the nations. His name was Abraham.

Abraham encountered a world that was far removed from G-d. A world where the spiritual was sacrificed for immediate gratification. A world where multiple gods were worshipped as long as they didn't require any morality and dignity. It was in this context that Abraham preached monotheism. He taught that the Almighty wanted us to be kind to others and live ethical lives.

Abraham was so successful that he attracted 100,000 people to the awareness and belief in One G-d and the Oneness of G-d. He brought the concept of G-dliness to the masses. Thus, Judaism was built on the foundation of outreach. For over 3,500 years Jews have made reaching out to our brothers and sisters a priority.

I have known Rabbi Dovid Asher for over twenty years since he was a young man who traveled to Israel on an outreach mission that I coordinated. He has always had a caring soul, thirsting to deliver the Almighty's Torah to Jews far and wide. In this book, Rabbi Asher brings the concept of Jewish outreach to life through the prism of the Torah.

I can't think of a topic more foundational to Judaism than the tool of outreach that Abraham used to build a global recognition of Hashem, which then led to the development of the Jewish people as a whole. Rabbi Asher will lead you on a spiritual journey that will enhance the quality of life for all Jews.

May the Almighty bless all of us with the strength and inspiration to connect His children to their Father.

ACKNOWLEDGMENTS

While it might be unusual to acknowledge one's elementary school when publishing a *sefer* as an adult, it certainly fits the chosen theme in that someone valued outreach enough to invest in a day-school in Allentown, Pennsylvania. The Jewish Day School and its constituency deserve credit for creating lifelong students dedicated to a healthy curiosity of Torah Judaism. The immediate credit, though, goes to Yeshivas Rabbeinu Yitzchak Elchonon and Keneseth Beth Israel of Richmond, Virginia.

For ten years, I had the glorious privilege of learning in the *beis midrash* system, often due to the wondrous generosity of Yeshiva University. Following secondary school years learning in Hebrew Academy of Nassau County, Kushner Yeshiva High School, and, ultimately, Rav Teitz Mesivta Academy, my parents enabled me to embark on a journey of rigorous *talmud Torah* at Yeshivat Shaarei Mevaseret Tziyon, Yeshiva University, Yeshivat Derech HaTalmud (Rav Ilson's), Marcos and Adina Katz Kollel, Gruss Kollel, and YU Torah Mitzion Kollel of Chicago, along with limited stints at Mir Yeshiva, Kollel Linas HaTzedek, Morasha Kollel, and Aish HaTorah. Special mention goes to NCSY for the absolutely vital, informal educational experiences that infused the passion and inspiration necessary to pursue these *mekomos kedushah*. Another special mention goes to Bostoner Chassidus, as Rav Levi Yitzchak Horowitz, *zt"l*, and his rebbitzen, Raichel Unger Leifer, *zt"l*, led my parents to a type of Torah lifestyle that brought me towards a life of Torah community service. Without them, I would not be here.

During this period of having the *zechus* of being *shivti b'veis Hashem*, Rav Azarya Berzon, *shlita*, introduced me to the world of *lomdus* and showed me that the beauty of the vastness of the *yam shel Torah* was without comparison as it illuminated the purpose of life itself. Specifically, Rabbi Shimon Isaacson and Rabbi Uri Pilichowski—along with too many others to adequately acknowledge—impressed upon me the profound truth that was, heretofore unbeknownst to me, a part of the *mehus* of my very definition. With the Mevaseret experience, it became my drive to pursue *shimush talmidei chachamim* of the highest caliber, in order to soak in as much *yesodei haTorah* and *yedios haTorah* in an effort to make sense of the meaning of life. Moments with Rav Elyashiv, *zt"l*; the second Bostoner Rebbe, *zt"l*; Rav Aharon Yehuda Leib Shteinman, *zt"l*; and, *yibadel lechayim tovim aruchim*, Rav Chaim Kanievsky, *shlita*, helped mold and shape my world outlook (*Eiruvin* 13b). More profoundly, the three and half years of study under my *rebbi muvhak*, HaRav Michoel Rosensweig, *shlita*, impressed upon me to try to view all of life through the prism of a unique *anivus* that could exclusively be cultivated with an absolute dedication to *yiras Shamayim*, which could only be wrought by *d'var Hashem*. In addition, my years of being a *talmid* of Rav Chaim Ilson, *shlita*, Rav Aharon Lichtenstein, *zt"l*, Rav Baruch Simon, *shlita*, Rav Hershel Schachter, *shlita*, Rav Mordechai Willig, *shlita*, Rav Assaf Bednarsh, *shlita*, Rav Avishai David, *shlita*, and countless others have left me in awe of the richness of our *mesorah*. With regard to this *sefer* and my life's ambition of imparting Torah as effectively as possible, Rav Noach Weinberg's, *zt"l*, impact on my family, my elder siblings, and on me through many hours of *yechidus* cannot be understated. I would be remiss to not thank Rabbi Kaddish Waldman, Rabbi Josh Blass, Rabbi Saul Zucker, Rabbi Chaim Marcus, Rabbi Shmuel Maybruch, and other *mashgichim* who helped guide me through the various mental health issues that often plague young *bochurim* as they navigate life.

Keneseth Beth Israel deserves a lion's share of gratitude as they risked assigning the role of Central Virginia's *mara d'asra* to an unproven *avreich*. It's certainly not simple entrusting, ennobling, and enabling a young *posek* to deal with local issues of *vaad ha'kashrus, eiruvin, chinuch, chevrah kadishah, askanus, mikvaos, beis hakvaros, kupos tzedakah,* and *inyanei chessed,* not to mention the basics such as pastoral care, daily *shailos, drashos,* and of course *shiurim.* Toward the end of nine years in Greater Richmond and into the tenth year, the congregation invested in a sabbatical for my family. These months allowed for the compilation and organization of my *he'aros* on the *parshiyos* from my tenure in the Katz Kollel. This *chibbur* had been in the making for more than a dozen years. There are not enough words to adequately thank my students and the *baal batim* for their contributions, as Chazal state, "*U'mitalmidai yoser mikulan.*" Special thanks are in order to our close *chaver,* Mr. Marcus Weinstein, for his financial support of numerous *klal* projects within the Richmond area and Eretz Yisrael. Thank you to Rav Yisrael Meir David for his editing as well.

The luxury of growing up as the child of my parents, *yibadel lechayim aruchim,* and my grandparents, *zichronam livrachah,* is indescribable. The *shevil ha'zahav,* the intellectualism, and the lessons of *yashrus* were replete from the years of childhood through today. My older siblings were the ultimate teachers, and my late eldest sister, Rebbetzin Elana Golda Rosenblatt, *z"l,* set the bar very high for all of us, including all of my extraordinary cousins, most notably Akiva Kolchin, who was a supreme role model for me while growing up.

Most importantly, my wife sacrificed her peace of mind so that I could write and commit these ideas to paper. Her grace in taking care of our family so that I can dedicate my energies to the Jewish People is the highest standard imaginable. When our sabbatical trip to Israel was cancelled last minute due to the pandemic and instead turned into several months of seeing the natural wonders of the United States, the *sefer* on *Maseches Beitzah* took a back seat to this *sefer,* and living out of our minivan for this road trip created unexpected pressures on the family, which were tackled miraculously by my wife. The term "grateful" is inadequate when describing my South Florida parents and grandparents for bringing this *eishes chayil* into my life. "*Sheli u'shelachem shelah hi!*"

Acharon Acharon Chaviv, the tears of *tefillah* and the dancing of *simchah* are but a small expression of acknowledging the ultimate reward of encountering "*diyukno*" *shel Avinu shebashayim*, as described on the sixth day of Creation. To be a part of "*anu ratzim*" is incomparably more lucrative than winning the lottery. With knowledge comes responsibility, so I ask Hakadosh Baruch Hu to bless Am Yisrael, and indeed all of us, in learning these *divrei Torah* within our *s'vivah* so that we might yet understand weekly that the opportunity of learning the Torah pales in comparison to learning Torah with a constant eye towards teaching Torah. As we state every day in the siddur that the ideal state of *talmud Torah* is "*lilmod u'lelamed*" in that learning it and sharing it go together, "*V'haarev na Hashem Elokeinu es divrei Torascha b'finu u'v'fi* ***amcha Beis Yisrael***."

INTRODUCTION

"A*m mefuzar u'meforad*" (a spread out and disjointed people among the nations) is our characterization and description from our historic enemy, Haman the *Amaleki*. The thesis and the purpose of this *sefer* is to provide ample substantiation that the future that we are meant to exemplify is a broader and a more wholly intact, fully integrated Am Yisrael than as currently exists. To understand the caliber of peoplehood to which we should aspire, we simply need to review the weekly Torah portion, which repeatedly underscores a national unity predicated upon a Torah lifestyle that embraces the widest and most expansive definition of Klal Yisrael.

The moment has arrived for us to question denominationalism as it currently exists. Being traditional Torah Jews means striving sincerely and energetically for an authenticity uniquely accompanied by the power of truth. What is at stake is seriously, yet simply, our continuity. We know that a faithful *emunah* and Jewish continuity are commensurate. Not radically, but in an intentionally driven manner, we need to face with honesty that the prospect of who we are versus who we could be as a people are polar opposites. The talents and skillsets of those not yet living in a Torah community, by which we mean every aspect of life is inspired by Torah, are desperately needed to help fight the onslaught of a debilitating secularism. In short, *galus* (exile) presents so many obstacles that we must have as many hands-on-deck as possible to assist with the improvement of the Jewish People.

Often, we find communities that are almost entirely homogenous, lacking opinions that vary, leading to a narrowness that precludes a healthy exchange of ideas. As the Gemara in *Taanis* relates, Rabbi Yochanon found the loss of Reish Lakish irreplaceable, and his own continued existence impossible, without a formidable intellectual adversary. While no one could responsibly suggest inviting heresy or apostasy into our institutions, closing ourselves off completely to outside ideas and failing to responsibly share the *hashkafas haTorah* is, likewise, similarly untenable. The advancement of Jewry requires an expansion of access to Torah. Outreach is not about saving another person as much as it is about having a flame in a room of darkness that one is willing to share out of pure generosity of spirit. This applies to different people in different contexts; some people might be spiritually stronger in certain areas and others within other areas. The more flames shared, the brighter the room. It is significantly painful for people not to be familiar with their own heritage and their own tradition. If one couples that fact with the notion that the Almighty is waiting to see if we truly wish to be in a world with the third Beis Hamikdash, and the kind of peace that's most conducive for Torah growth, then the urgency will be readily apparent. Therefore, we cannot continue to set up our shuls and schools in a way that subliminally, or sometimes even overtly, precludes less affiliated Jews who are in our midst from taking part in our precious *mesorah*.

Recently, the term "*kiruv*" has perhaps rightfully come under fire as a controversial term. After all, who can speak with an audacious certainty that he knows which mortal is closer to the *Borei Olam*? Most importantly, though, we need to understand that our family and our *chiyuvim mitzad areivus* are incomplete without higher levels of participation across the board. If our numbers of consistent weekly shul and daily Judaic school attendance remain below 15 percent of the total Jewish American population, then an untold number of potential future successes will remain *out of reach* (based on recent studies by Avi Chai, Pew, etc.). We would certainly be more deserving to have a worldwide ingathering, referred to as the *geulah sheleimah*, should we be able to model coming together ourselves within our own cities at least in some improved way!

There is a different angle that is even more uncomfortable for us to consider. Are those of us who were raised or who were given the experience of authentic Torah living—replete with Shabbos observance and the culture that comes along with Torah ideals—appreciative enough to recognize the privilege and the related responsibility it endows? As the Chafetz Chaim alludes to many times throughout his works, if a person has the medical knowledge to provide healthcare, or if a person has the firefighting skills to extinguish a fire, then should he not employ his prowess to help others? Whether we consider the mitzvah of *lo saamod al dam rei'echa* (not stand idly by your brother's blood) or the Mishnayos discussing the category of the Avtinas family, as will be discussed in the coming pages, our entire tradition enjoins us to utilize the gifts we were given by the Almighty to better the world around us. These gifts of a Torah education, mitzvah living, and Shabbos observance are privileged currency that we ought to invest for a more robust Torah society. We are meant to enlist our unique opportunities for the sake of showing others that the Almighty has endowed us with a system to answer most of life's queries. Keeping it to ourselves is equivalent to denying others Torah insights and experiences, which is a kind of harsh cruelty, unless, *chas v'shalom,* we view such noble differentiation as insignificant. Put simplistically, if one held a bank note for his next-door neighbor worth millions of dollars, yet failed to inform him of its whereabouts, then we would view that as ethically bereft. *L'havdil elef havdalos*, we ought to apply this example to the invaluable *Torah Hakedoshah*, the ultimate *yerushah* and *morashah* from our ancestors. So, we should ask ourselves: Is it our lack of *emunah*, our lack of *chashivus haTorah*, our extreme distraction, or our callousness towards our brothers and sisters that prevents us from the *kiyum* (fulfillment) regarding such accountability?

Moreover, how many accomplishments have we seen, and how many *toldos* have been created, because of welcoming interactions between ordinary people who happen to come from different Jewish backgrounds. The working theory here is that the *chochmas haTorah* contains a binding understanding that if two people focus together on serving the Almighty, both will be fundamentally changed for the better. There will be a mutual enhancement that will leave both parties in a better place, regardless of what the specifics might look like. The imagery of *aish haTorah* is that, unlike most materials, when one shares fire then the original source of fire is not diminished, yet it adds further and ever-expanding illumination. It is not a black-and-white proposition that a specific observance will knowingly lead to a known level of religiosity. Rather, it is the general understanding that striving for goodness, as established by the Almighty, is the duty of all mankind. This composition, through the weekly *divrei Torah*, seeks to ask that question and to review whether we believe strongly enough in what we practice to want to impart Torah to others.

The purpose of this *sefer* is to establish a faith of strong conviction that the weekly *sidrah* emphasizes how our leaders and our mitzvos help us to internalize the preciousness of every opportunity to further imbue the world with a sense of *kavod Shamayim,* especially those within Klal Yisrael. We might have neither the *kochos* nor the exceptional stamina to be a Moshe Rabbeinu, but, as the *Rambam* details, we are all born with such comparable latent potential. Despite being unable to effect change like many of our heroes and progenitors, as Chazal relate to us, we are nevertheless not free to desist from attempting to raise the stature of *sheim Hashem.* Indeed, as we recite in *Hallel*, the purpose of the daily rising of the sun is, "*mehullal sheim Hashem,*" which means to praise the Almighty, or rather to make Hashem's name praiseworthy. Interestingly, the context of David HaMelech's words refer to Hashem's stature among the general population of the world. Naturally, one might posit that a prerequisite for global communication of Hashem's omnipotence would be first and foremost our own people's meaningful, more extensive appreciation of *d'var Hashem.*

We are commanded to love Hashem, and it is axiomatic that we express our love—a love found within our hearts—not only to ourselves, but also to others. Like Avraham, we are also sought to spread this love and gratitude to others by thinking strategically about what would be most effective in helping people gain a certain kind of clarity, which is only attainable via Torah.

As the joke goes, a couple walks into the office of their marital therapist, and the therapist inquires about the issue at hand. The wife complains that the husband never tells her that he loves her. The therapist turns to the husband for explanation. The husband defends himself by saying that he told her that he loved her at their wedding and if anything changes then he would make sure to let her know! The therapist, of course, then explains that that is not how it works, and reiterating a statement of love is part of a healthy marriage.

So, we must ask ourselves, are we in a good marriage with the Almighty? As the experience of Har Sinai was our chuppah, and we proclaimed our unwavering devotion with the words "*naaseh v'nishma*," so are we today in this same standard of adoration? Will we be condemned by our own conscience and by the Almighty for communicating loyalty to so many other isms and aspects of life, yet foregoing showcasing similar expressions for our Creator? Like on Seder night, when we recite the *Hallel*, there is a reenactment of the spontaneous joy of surviving the splitting of the sea while being ultimately saved from our vicious slave owners; do we not possess moments when we are overly restrained and reserved to our own detriment with a failure to launch praises of gratitude even in these modern times?

We are meant to have the courage to acknowledge the endowment of *kedushah* instilled within us that comes with a unique mission. The all-important mitzvah of sanctifying Hashem's name presumes that our existence is for that purpose, and that this mitzvah is actionable as a furtherance of *emunah* within our respective societies. The *Rambam* in *Deos* calls on us not to be fearful of some sort of presumed inhibitions wrought by excessive insecurities based of our non-Jewish environs and neighbors. We can't be scared by those around us to do the right thing. This emphasis on interconnection is manifested through halachic observance. The *din* is that it's best for a Jewish family to share their oil and wicks while lighting a single candle each of the eight nights of Chanukah rather than their Jewish friend not lighting that night at all. It is better to make Kiddush several times for those who need to hear it rather than being concerned about excessively invoking Hashem's name. Similarly, it is preferable to share *dalet minim* on Sukkos with a neighbor, and gift our set to another, rather than keeping a set for ourselves. Our interconnection in history and legal philosophy is not abstract, but tangibly real, as found throughout the details of halachah.

Perhaps, the leading argument for communal self-reflection, as we plot a wider and broader and more unified Torah community, is the Torah's adjuring us to see beyond our separate and distinct superficialities toward a binding spiritual oneness. Our sages teach us that if we are obligated to be involved in saving physical lives whenever possible, then *kol shekein*, a person's limitless spiritual lifespan is required to be salvaged. The mitzvah of returning a lost object maintains an outlook that we are our "brother's keeper" because being on the same team means having each other's back. One's material diminishment is our responsibility as *metzuvim*—not just because of an awesome shared history and destiny, but also because of a profound ideology that presupposes separateness as antithetical to our collective Torah persona. Chazal tell us that vengeance upon our fellow Jew is as irrational as the left hand taking revenge against the right hand that had accidentally severed the left hand's finger. This timeless teaching is not using dramatics for the purposes of an over-the-top exhortation. It is *pshat*. It is the accurate depiction of what should be the outlook and approach of our people.

The *Talmud Yerushalmi* understands the last curse in the *tochachah* to mean that those who are in a position to fortify the stature of Torah, yet fail to allocate their resources for the achievable means of strengthening Torah, will have all their good deeds and righteousness count for naught as they will be grouped with the accursed. Affirming such in the positive was Yoshiyahu HaMelech, who wished to absolve himself from idolatrous complicity and stated two of the most famous words in our history, "*alai l'hakim*," which means that it is on me to raise it up. Yoshiyahu understood the unbounded political power he possessed as king. He pronounced these words to signal a new era of looking in the mirror with the intention of seeking change. Today, we often cite societal trends of decreasing Jewish involvement and mitigated communal thriving. Truth be told, the best hope for achieving accomplishment for the sake of Torah is not writing or talking about what is wrong, but rather personal accountability. In other words, if I want to see a better tomorrow for the Torah, then how can I most effectually transmit my own deep Torah love and my own heartfelt convictions to others? This *sefer* seeks to instill weekly messages of ownership for the path toward progress for Torah enrichment within our communities and their institutions.

The *Chovos Halevavos* writes that the greatest person in the world, who actualizes his potential to the highest levels and comes closest to his Creator due to his tremendous merits, pales in comparison to those who teach others the necessary path of goodness (*Chovos Halevavos, Shaar Asiri, Shaar Ahavas Hashem* 6:16). Our Torah has always called on us to focus our attention and our efforts beyond ourselves. Perfection of oneself without efforts to help and guide others is, by definition, not perfection. Our patriarch, Avraham Avinu, was not necessarily the most devout individual of his era but was rather the most cherished by the Almighty because of his ability to make others around him better. He helped others get the most out of life and, for this reason, he was selected. At the end of Avraham's life, the Torah uses the word "*v'savea*," which means "and he was satisfied." This is the only such usage. His satisfaction came from the notion that, more so than all other Biblical personalities, Avraham utilized his G-d-given gifts to help others gain the clarity that he worked so desperately to achieve. Avraham listened to the truth of the universe for the sake of sharing that wealth of knowledge with those around him.

An oft mentioned teaching of Rav Noach Weinberg, as told by his disciple Rabbi Shraga Simmons, echoing the words of Rabbeinu Bachya Ibn Pakuda's *Chovos Halevavos*, goes as follows:

> *The Dubno Maggid explains this point with the following parable: There was a wealthy man who reached the age of seventy and decided to make a celebration. He sent a letter to his two sons living in another country that said, "I want you and your families to celebrate with me. Do not be concerned with the expenses, because anything that you spend in my honor, I will give back to you twenty times. If you spend one thousand dollars, I will give you twenty thousand dollars. If you spend twenty thousand dollars, I'll give you four hundrend thousand dollars."*

The older son was a man of means. After hearing the offer, he went out and bought the nicest carriage, the nicest clothes for his children, a new shtreimel for himself, and jewels for his wife—because he knew that the more he'd spend, the more he'd get back.

Dressed in all their finery, they began their journey to his father's home. On the way, he passed the house of his younger brother, who was a poor fellow with no money at all. He could not even borrow money, because no one would give him credit. Suddenly, his wealthy brother appeared and he said to the poor brother, "Aren't you coming?"

The poor brother answered, "I have no money to rent a carriage."

"No problem. Gather your family, and you will travel in mine." So, the poor brother, with his family, climbed into the carriage and off they went to the party: the older brother's family in their finery, and the younger son's family in patched and worn-out clothes.

At the grand party, the older brother approached his father and said, "I spent fifty thousand dollars for this party, so, according to your offer, I am entitled one million dollars."

The father looked at him and said, "I'm not giving you a penny."

"What do you mean?" asked his son. "A deal is a deal!"

"I said that anything you spend to honor me, I'll give you back twenty times. But you didn't spend this money for my honor; you spent it for your own honor. If you were really concerned with honoring me, then you would have taken care of your younger brother as well."

When telling this story, Rav Noach would pound his fist and say: "It's a chillul Hashem (desecration of G-d's Name) of historic proportions. How do we even raise our heads? In America alone, over one million Jews do not identify themselves as Jewish. Do you think they found these alternatives more enlightening than our Torah, or were they so ignorant

> *of their own heritage that non-Jewish society reached them without a fight? We left our brothers to die! What are we going to answer to the Almighty?"*
>
> *Rav Noach would conclude: "If you are concerned with the Almighty's honor, you need to care for his children who are spiritually impoverished. By doing so, you will be entitled to the most profound reimbursement possible!"*

The Dubno Maggid is sharing with us that the whole Torah, which guides towards a life of service, is also meant to underscore that commitment without empowering others is not comparable to tying one's future and fortunes to his fellow. At the very least, we'll be asked to justify why our efforts didn't match the intensity and the passion of our most ardent enemies and detractors. Torah individuals living in the West are uniquely positioned to take the faith to the people. We understand that seeing is believing and that today's skepticism will make faith nearly impossible for those who find great convenience in ignoring G-d's existence. We know that our *mesorah* is based on a teaching of Rambam that Jews believe in a Higher Being not because of miracles, like the splitting of the sea and the ten plagues in Mitzrayim, but rather because of the physical presence of our ancestors at Har Sinai. At present, leaps of faith are not en vogue, and sharing our unique opinion of valuing verifiable evidence is quite inspiring. Fleets of inspiration are inadequate for deepening conviction and fostering belief. It is the intention herein to display arguments for effective devotion to a disciplined approach for widening the umbrella of our communities.

The challenge in writing a themed *sefer* on the weekly *sidrah* is that Torah is not Torah unless it is accurate. If a person has an agenda and then looks at the *pesukim*, then one is liable to make a mistake in correctly interpreting the Almighty's message. It is critical to make sure the *mesorah* is transmitted accurately, because otherwise it's not our *mesorah* and will lack the power to make the necessary impact of creating higher-quality *avodas Hashem*. It is our timeless *chachamim* and *mefarshim* who communicate with their own words the important role outreach plays in the development of *Yahadus*. Without the *ro'ei Yisrael* (shepherds of Israel) and the heroes of our Torah taking responsibility for representing Torah values to others, we would not be here today with the communities that we have. By formulating these messages systematically and with modern application, then one is able to make these verities actionable for the sake of the surrounding society. Living within a neighborhood, by definition, creates certain moral tasks and, by learning the *parashah* more closely, we can tell that Torah outreach is one such responsibility.

Unfortunately, many of the Jews around us just see the Torah as another book on the market and do not even admit the Divine origin of authorship. There is a direct correlation between quality of Judaic education and these beliefs. The less substantive education, the more doubts of faith that exist. One simply needs to increase Torah discourse with those who have not been as fortunate to be brought up with an understanding that the Torah comes from G-d. So many of life's challenges can be helped with these deeper, mutual, and jointly shared understandings.

We are all bound together by a common history, and that miraculous history of our endurance is widely appreciated, yet not frequently seen as connected to the point of differentiation, which is specifically the Torah's imprint. Our eternality is unique because we are unique as determined by our Har Sinai moment. Exceptional ire for the Jew throughout the world is Divine proof of the conscientiousness and burdensome yoke that we represent to the world around us. How painful it must be to not understand why hatred is spewed limitlessly in our direction! Our numeric paucity ought to provide little discomfort to others, but our cause célèbre of G-dliness drives an irrational angst that, often, even results in violence. There is no greater evidence to this than the international condemnations repeatedly slung at the State of Israel as it represents the actual and the proverbial Jew.

The world's animosity of the Jew often stems from those who want to live life without having one's instincts and desires harnessed. In part, outreach is about helping all Jews see the soulful abilities that allow one to soar past more basic animalistic limitations. Outreach is about actualizing the potential bestowed upon mankind at Creation. So much of the shortcomings of civilization were wrought by manmade, artificially created morality without serious consideration given to objective morality. Ethical relativism can be stifled with a broader communal learning of a G-d-centric driven code of behavior and the directly related Torah studying activities that have been part of our people forever. We need to overcome taking the easier route of settling for a private experience rather than a collective observational experience by pointing out the vastness and the immaculate beauty of the physical world around us having not occurred by chance, rather through a Creator.

In consultation with *ro'ei Yisrael*, we need to openly discuss worldly topics, like women's issues for instance, and how the Torah was the entity responsible for giving rights to women and empowering them via the formal institution of marriage, thereby establishing consent as a prerequisite and ensuring financial remuneration should marriages not work out. We need to talk about how pain is not the opposite of joy, and how extreme comfort is actually a great contributor to eventual pain. We need to talk about how man's limited scope often precludes the understanding of why certain events take place. Contrarily, but not contradictedly, we also need to wonder aloud what would have happened if there would have never been the original Egyptian exile of the Children of Israel, and what we would be like as a nation without the travails that characterized so much of our past. We need to converse with others about the Torah's growth philosophy of not worrying about what we cannot control and instead focusing on what additional potential lies within, and then to consider what this all portends concerning human dignity and the gift of life itself. All the while, we must promote the idea that none of the above has value unless we internalize the lesson of *bechirah chafshis* (free will). This is a lesson of empowerment—that we are not shackled by mitzvos, but rather that mitzvos facilitate an unleashing of our power to overcome initial inclinations for a more robust end-goal of an intentional, more widespread greater good.

These *parshiyos*, as analyzed in the coming pages, drive home the point that we cannot live Jewishly without an outlook of a broader tradition and a more Torah-inclusive perspective. We need to honor what we do on a weekly basis by adding intention to our Torah living. By focusing exclusively inward, we then miss out on a more robust Jewish experience. The charitable experience of giving Torah is not a material one; rather it's the greatest way to add to our spiritual bottom line via extending our spiritual selves beyond our own *dalet amos*. Let us all strive to match the challenge set forth by Rav Moshe Feinstein, *zt"l*, in years past to tithe our energies for outreach (*Igros Moshe*, *Even Ha'ezer* 4:26). If all those with the luxuries of enriched Torah experiences give 10 percent of their *kochos* toward connecting with others who lack the knowledge and resources of Jewish life, then surely, we will merit a *geulah sheleimah* based on the quantity and the quality of the force of our combined merits.

While the introduction is intended to be read separately, the following *divrei Torah* are meant to be a regular reminder, rooted in *talmud Torah* of the *Chumash*, that a unified Klal Yisrael predicated upon oneness is fundamentally mightier than a disparate and disjointed one. May Hashem bless our learning of the weekly *sidrah* with a sensitivity and a keener awareness of the role we play within the greater totality of the Almighty's people!

SEFER BEREISHIS

BEREISHIS

A fundamental question for any student of life to ask is, "Why did G-d create the world?" Surely, G-d knew that the introduction of anything physical into His world would necessarily introduce limitation and imperfection. Why did He not simply allow the nonphysical entity to continue to exist, serene and free of interference by imperfect beings?

By creating the world the way He did, Hashem teaches us that without contrast, there is no perspective. Without darkness, light is not seen. Without sickness, health is not appreciated. Without runners-up, there are no champions. The same is true with spirituality; devoid of physicality, spirituality cannot be perceived in the world. Therefore, physicality and spirituality are not the opponents we perceive them to be; rather, they work together. Much of life is about figuring out the right balance of such elements.

The Avtinas and Garmu families (*Yoma* 3:3) were illustrious in Jewish society during the times of the Beis Hamikdash. They were the families of Kohanim responsible for the incense and the showbread, respectively. They used their specialized knowledge of the raw product and an optimal manufacturing process to monopolize the market so that the administration could go nowhere else to procure these necessary items for the Beis Hamikdash. In the end, when the families died out, there was no one left to create the proper incense and showbread. Their hoarding of trade secrets upon which the community depended was considered reprehensible. The Mishnah in *Yoma* states that they were in violation of a basic Jewish value, as captured by the words in *Mishlei*, "*kol paal Hashem lemaaneihu*," that all Divine creations are for Hashem. As Creator, G-d owns everything, and to hold a community hostage through selfish behavior is an affront to the purpose of Creation.

Some defend the Avtinas and Garmu families by suggesting that they simply did not want the information to fall into the wrong hands and for any alterations to be made. However, as the *Meiri* (1249–1310) explains, regardless of intentions, we must not sacrifice potential *kiddush Hashem* because of potential *chillul Hashem*. The *Ralbag* (1288–1344) explains that the previously quoted *pasuk* in *Mishlei*, "*Kol paal Hashem lemaaneihu*," is referring to the Creation of humanity, but it naturally follows that all *actions* of humanity need to also be for G-d. These noble families failed to ask themselves if they were truly motivated by pure intentions or inappropriate self-interest.

These priestly families should have known of the basic Jewish value found at the end of *Pirkei Avos*: "*Kol ma she'bara Hakadosh Baruch Hu b'olamo, lo vera'o ela l'chvodo*," that all G-dly creations are not for individual advancement but rather for a more widespread awareness of the Almighty. Considering the way that the *chachamim* treated the Avtinas and Garmu families for not disclosing just one aspect of our tradition, we must learn from them to share as much of Torah as possible. Just like they were meant to share their knowledge, the Torah as a whole is the highest level of knowledge and is certainly meant to be shared. The entire purpose of physical creations in *Parashas Bereishis* is to honor Hashem and to allow for widespread *kiddush Hashem* within our communities. Our learning can be elevated through living our Torah teachings and sharing them more broadly with those around us.

NOACH

At the very beginning of *Parashas Noach*, Noach is uniquely praised. He is labeled a *tzaddik*, yet this compliment is qualified by an asterisk of sorts when this same *pasuk* states, "*b'dorosav*" (in his generation). According to one approach, Noach was righteous but only in comparison to the rest of his generation, which was so evil that it had to be destroyed. It was certainly an accomplishment to achieve *tzidkus* status despite all the *rishus* surrounding him daily. In contrast, it seems quite embarrassing for the Torah to so openly refer to Noach's greatness as being limited.

Rashi elaborates that not only was Noach just considered great relative to the immorality around him, but had he lived ten generations later during the times of Avraham Avinu, he would have amounted to nothing at all! He would have been neither a *navi* nor a *tzaddik*. Moreover, Chazal specifically tell us the same is true had he lived during the times of Moshe or Shmuel. The *Emes L'Yaakov* wants to know why our sages specified these three individuals. What was unique about these Jewish leaders? What did Avraham, Moshe, and Shmuel represent?

Rav Yaakov Kamenetsky explains that these three individuals represented a type of leadership that successfully improved society around them. They helped Torah permeate the lives of multiple generations. Their influence and strategy enabled their interactions with others to inspire higher, more meritorious levels of observance. Noach took care of the animals effectively, yet even those actions were only due to the explicit directions from the Almighty. The *Ramban* (1194–1270) states that the reason behind the miracle of all the animals fitting into the Ark was in order to facilitate a conversation between the gawkers and Noach so that he could draw them nearer to a more ethical way of life, thereby preventing the flood. Rav Kamenetsky elaborates that if Noach would have been a *tzaddik gamur*, then his reproach of his neighbors would have made an impact. Unfortunately, he was so wrapped up in his own life that he never took the time to get to know his community, and, therefore, he never learned how to communicate with them properly.

Rav Moshe Feinstein makes a similar point based on the word "*tamim*," which refers to Noach's completeness as an individual. By contrasting the definitions of *tamim* and *tzaddik*, we will be able to better grasp the underlying message of Noach, who paled in comparison to other great leaders in our history. The wording of this week's opening line teaches us that the Almighty wanted Noach to be objectively righteous as indicated by "*ish tzaddik*," but he was not perfect, as alluded to by "*tamim hayah b'dorosav*." In other words, Hashem wanted Noach to be more involved with the people. Jewish leaders cannot accomplish as much as they are supposed to if they are overly reclusive. There needs to be the right balance of working on oneself while simultaneously being connected to the people. Rav Feinstein suggests that Noach did not satisfy that obligation, and he is remembered for that shortcoming.

Many of us are concerned about sharing our lives with those who do not align themselves with Torah ideals. We may think it will negatively impact us and our families. This introductory *pasuk* compels us to look confidently towards Avraham, Moshe, and Shmuel as the paragons for representing our *hashkafos*, as opposed to Noach whose greatness was qualified at the very beginning of "his" *sidrah*.

LECH LECHA

In this week's *parashah*, Avraham is told to leave his birthplace and to go to the place that Hashem will show him. The composition of Hashem's instruction is a bit odd. Why specify that Avraham must go out to the land of Canaan (12:1), when, clearly, he has to leave Charan, his place of origin, in order to get to the destination selected by Hashem? What is the significance of telling Avraham to go to the land of Canaan?

Yeshayahu HaNavi tells us, "*Chasdei Hashem azkir*," that the *chessed* of Hashem is recalled. The referenced acts of *chessed* are the existential interventions that allowed Jewish history to continue. Our existence as a nation is the ultimate merciful *chessed*. In this week's *sidrah*, the followers of Avraham and Sarah are referred to as their products, "*es hanefesh asher asu b'Charan*." We can deduce that, while in advance of the journey to leave their idolatrous birthplace behind, Avraham and Sarah had a lot of meaningful conversations. The result of these many conversations was that they didn't leave alone; an entourage of devotees and disciples followed Avraham and Sarah out of Charan. As the Gemara in *Sanhedrin* (19b) states, "those who teach Torah to others instill life within them." The insights gained through Torah pedagogy lead one to different realms of understanding about the world.

The *Rambam* (1138–1204) details how Avraham and Sarah could not contain their enthusiasm for the Almighty. They were bursting with excitement and simply had to share their discovery of the true nature of the Creator. Avraham and Sarah successfully led thousands of people to transcend the status quo to achieve greatness. This could not have happened without going "out" and taking responsibility for the ultimate *chessed* of helping people gain perspective on life itself, thereby providing an otherwise unattainable daily clarity of purpose. Sharing this perspective was a kindness that could never be paid back in full. G-d forbid that they keep it all to themselves!

(As an important aside, we do not know the names of Avraham's and Sarah's disciples, thereby highlighting that Hashem praises helping others with such advancement, even if it's only temporary and limited.)

A common and understandable reaction to this commentary is that you and I are not comparable to our Avos and Imahos. Surely, they were successful because of their unique talents and abilities. While we may all recognize that reaching out to our fellow Jew is an important task for ourselves and for our community, where does it rank when time is limited and there are so many other responsibilities? Would it not be better to take care of our responsibilities at home rather than go out to engage those in the world around us?

The Chafetz Chaim explains that with an extensive presence in the diaspora comes a damaging assimilation. Assimilation is a kind of urgent crisis. If, *chas v'shalom,* we see our fellow bleeding to death without anyone else around to help, then certainly we would do all we could to save his life without hesitating due to a lack of training. Just like Hashem saved our lives and Avraham created life through his teaching, those privileged to have Torah must share it with others. Rav Chaim Volozhin takes this even further when describing how the pain of a parent watching a child writhing in pain from an injury is actually harder for the parent than for the child. Similarly, the Almighty is "pained" by the spiritual struggles of even the most distant within Am Yisrael. Like Avraham and Sarah, the optimal way of fulfilling the mitzvah of *ahavas Hashem* is when one's love reaches a tipping point—recognizing how profound a life of Torah truly is—that he absolutely feels that he must share it with others.

Finally, the *Avudraham* elucidates the *Sim Shalom* prayer in *Shemoneh Esreh* by explaining that the words "*toras chayim*" follows references to "*tovah, u'verachah, chein v'chessed*" (goodness, blessing, grace, and kindness). He says the source for this is in *Devarim*, when Hashem tells us "*Ki hi chayecha v'orech yamecha*," that Torah is synonymous with life. In other words, living one's life fully means living in accordance with Torah, with the words of the Almighty who provides life. Let us recognize that the gift of life is the ultimate gift, and it supersedes many of our other responsibilities that often distract us from sharing *Toras Chayim*.

VAYEIRA

The Jewish People stand on the merits of our Avos and our Imahos. By learning from their actions, we can make *maasei avos siman l'banim* come alive. Avraham plants an "*eishel*" in Beer Sheva, and *Rashi* tells us that there is a debate as to whether an *eishel* is a tree or an inn. Either way, it is apparent that the *eishel* was a place for people to gather, and there they would learn the concepts of Hashem. As the *pasuk* states (21:33), they would learn how to call out to G-d. They would work on their relationship with their Creator, and they would learn to place their faith in Hashem instead of idols.

Since the Torah never includes irrelevant information, the *eishel* must be uniquely important. The *Ramban* details the content of those philosophical conversations at the *eishel*. Travelers were engaged in discussion on topics of time, origins of food, and religion. Avraham would enable them to see for themselves that only a G-d outside of time and space could have created the world around them.

The *eishel* was not just a place for teaching, but it was also a place of prayer. *Onkelos* comments on the words, "*Vayikra sham b'sheim Hashem*—And he called there in the name of G-d," that *Vayikra* refers to prayer. This explanation supports the idea that a place of learning is also an ideal place for davening. In the merit of Avraham reaching out to his fellow man, his prayers were answered at the *eishel* as indicated by the last verse in the twenty-first *perek* where the Torah emphasizes that he was granted the blessing of dwelling peacefully for many years.

Every day during *Aleinu*, we ask Hashem for a future where the world will unite in directing their requests to Him. When we state the words "*kol b'nei basar yikreu b'shmecha*," let it be a call to action. We must not sit back and wait for widespread knowledge of Hashem to happen. We need to be proactive like Avraham and Sarah and work towards that goal. They acted with intention. Chazal tell us that when Avraham and Sarah's guests would rise to leave and thank their hosts, the response would be to instead be thankful to the Creator who brought the world into existence so that they could take part in it and all the wondrous delicacies made by the Almighty. The Gemara tells us that it is not Avraham who "called out," as per the literal translation, but rather that his actions led others to call out to Hashem, most likely for the first time.

Ultimately, the *pasuk* teaches us that the *eishel* was the means by which "*vayikra*" could take place. Once Avraham taught others to praise Hashem, that teaching, in itself, became a kind of prayer, and the *eishel* was transformed into a kind of shul that served as an open tent for all to come to a true understanding of a Torah lifestyle (*Midrash Shochar Tov, Tehillim* 110). Just like a shul today is a gathering point for acknowledging the Almighty's presence, so too, the *eishel* served that very purpose as well. The power of the *eishel* and the example of Avraham forces us to consider what outposts we might be able to create that enable frank, enriching discussion concerning Torah living.

CHAYEI SARAH

It is no secret that Sarah Imeinu lived a life of great hardship. She suffered through decades of barrenness, experienced family dysfunction, and then had to leave all that she knew for the unfamiliar. One would expect this all to take a great toll on her. However, Chazal tell us that as a prophetess, she was the greatest of her era, even greater than her husband. How could it be that Avraham, who led the intellectual revolution and turned so many minds toward the Almighty, was not at least on the same level as his wife, Sarah?

According to the *Netziv* (1816–1893), Avraham was so busy working to build a strong spiritual movement that he was more distracted from his personal relationship with Hashem than Sarah was. We ought to consider that Avraham knew the impact that his outreach efforts would have on his own relationship with Hashem, and yet he pursued these objectives regardless of this outcome.

Similarly, Mordechai was so involved in preserving the Jewish community in Shushan and lobbying Achashveirosh's government for basic religious rights that he, naturally, spent much time away from his Torah studies due to the severe political vulnerabilities. The Gemara in *Megillah* (16b) tells us that this resulted in his colleagues demoting him in the Sanhedrin. Of course, Mordechai knew that his public service would result in somewhat of an erosion of his Torah expertise, but he importantly recognized that the times called for him to act for the sake of Am Yisrael. Moshe Rabbeinu was also brought down spiritually because of his involvement with the leadership of the Jewish People. His dream and original "destiny" to enter the land of Israel was denied as a result of his anger evoked by Klal Yisrael in the *midbar.* Comparisons to such giant leaders can be very helpful in revealing the impact an environment can have on an individual.

Every Shabbos morning, we acknowledge the special place and the unique gifts of those who work for the common good and welfare of others. We say, "*v'kol mi she'oskim b'tzarchei tzibbur b'emunah Hakadosh Baruch Hu yeshaleim secharam.*" Why do we acknowledge weekly the unique standing of public servants with a special *mishabeirach* as opposed to teachers, scholars, or *roshei yeshiva*? The answer is that those who work with Torah directly will certainly receive benefits, but for those busy tending to Hashem's children, the natural order needs to be changed via an intervention, and a miracle takes place. In other words, individuals typically get results based on the amount of effort they put in, but here Hashem provides above and beyond the ordinary. Indeed, there is unique reward and blessing bestowed on those who take time out of their own schedules, even Torah learning schedules, to assist others. Accordingly, the congregation is expected to take time out every Shabbos morning to focus on their gratitude for these public servants, thereby highlighting the unique role of these servants and their precious contributions to the *klal.*

The Jewish People are called children of the Almighty, as it states in *Devarim*, "*Banim Atem l'Hashem Elokeichem.*" Certainly, if we look after Hashem's children, then Hashem will look after us, and we should have *bitachon* that Hashem will grant us this just reward. Such noble diversion and idealistic distraction will not cause deficiency but will rather lift us up. Let us follow the example of Mordechai, Moshe, and Avraham who knowingly sacrificed some of their own personal Torah for the sake of keeping the Jewish people intact (*Yerushalmi*, *Berachos* 5:1). In our age of rampant assimilation and Jewish illiteracy, let us take time to reflect on how the teachings of our *sidrah* call on us to take more collective responsibility.

TOLDOS

The midrash (*Esther Rabbah* 8:1) tells us that the Purim story happened as a result of the conflict between Eisav and Yaakov. While it may be hard for us to see the direct connection between these two scenarios, we recognize that Eisav held on to a very real and constant antagonism for his brother, Yaakov, for having taken the birthright. This feeling was passed down from generation to generation within Eisav's family.

Rav Henoch Leibowitz explains that the only reason Haman was able to get so close to annihilating Yaakov Avinu's descendants in Shushan was because Yaakov failed to feel the pain of his brother. Yaakov did what he was supposed to do, but it was with the wrong mentality. Unquestionably, Yaakov made the right choice by listening to his mother, Rivkah Imeinu, and Hashem wanted him to receive the firstborn blessing. However, Yaakov was guilty for his lack of sensitivity towards Eisav. Eisav was evil, but he too had hopes and dreams.

This theme continues when Chazal suggest that Shechem attacked Dinah because Yaakov hid Dinah at his reunion with his brother Eisav after returning from years of exile. Again, we know that Yaakov acted correctly, but he failed to appreciate the positive impact that Dinah could have potentially had on Eisav's family. It certainly would have been tragic for Eisav to marry Dinah. However, Yaakov was neither sensitive to nor pained enough by the missed opportunity of having a more positive influence on his brother's life.

Rav Chaim Shmuelevitz (1902–1979) was known to tell the students of Mir that they were not true *b'nei Torah* if they didn't lose sleep as a result of the plights of the Jewish People. Perhaps at this very moment that you are reading this *d'var Torah*, you are not able to do anything for Am Yisrael. However, just like Yaakov needed to increase his overall sensitivity, we must improve our own mindset accordingly as well. Rav Leibowitz concludes by stating that we all need to work towards bringing our brothers and sisters closer to their heritage. And, if for some reason that isn't possible, we should at least be pained that so many Jews are estranged from Judaism and a life of mitzvos so that when the time comes, we'll be ready to act on our cultivated sensitivities.

VAYETZEI

In this week's *sidrah*, we see a rather extreme example of looking out for the spiritual well-being of another when Rachel Imeinu steals the idols of Lavan. It seems that her parting gift was an attempt to rob her family of their religion. Was Rachel motivated by hatred for deviant worship or by a love for her father?

The *Chasam Sofer* (1762–1839) writes that to "love thy neighbor" means to care about his spiritual well-being. Looking out for another's physical and financial well-being is also one of the *taryag mitzvos*. Chazal compare a parent to a teacher in that a parent gives a child life in *Olam Hazeh*, and a teacher gives a child life in *Olam Haba*. Being part of a loving relationship means more than simply meeting the basic necessities like food, clothing, and shelter. It also means supporting someone by sharing Torah and infusing meaning into shared interactions.

Rav Moshe Feinstein explains that as Yaakov finally reentered the land of Israel with his family after many years of exile, he did so rather quietly. Despite being enormously wealthy and extremely well-known, Yaakov came back to settle in his homeland with little fanfare. Based on this idea, Rav Moshe Feinstein says that in previous centuries, Jews were righteous or were at least in close proximity to righteousness and prophecy. He adds that today this is sadly not the case, and those who observe the Torah's edicts and follow in its ways need to publicize its critical messages. Rav Moshe says we ought to broadcast our values to ensure their preservation within mankind. This exemplifies the notion that to truly love someone means to help guide them, and not simply to live and let live. We have to work hard to strike the right balance in caring for our fellow Jews.

How do we know what the right balance is? We learn this by looking at the Torah obligation of giving *tochachah* (reproach). The mitzvah has an important caveat that reproach is prohibited if the individual will not be receptive. If there will be negative consequences and the person will be offended while being firmly attached to his wrongdoing, then it is best to forego the reproach. In other words, the rebuker must be very careful not to speak or to act in a way that will result in the opposite of the intended outcome. This is a very difficult demand of the Torah. The Torah expects us to think long and hard about the right course of action, since the stakes are exceedingly high. If it is the right setting, then we must gently guide our fellow; if not, then we must desist from possibly exacerbating the situation.

We can now see that Rachel was motivated by her affection for her father as per the Torah's concept of love, described by Rav Moshe and the *Chasam Sofer*. Our righteous matriarch certainly knew that a person needs to interact out of love more so than zealotry. She had thought, albeit mistakenly, that now was her chance to try and to separate her parents from idolatry. If the Torah wanted us to defend the honor of the mitzvos, then we would have to object to every transgression and give *tochachah* on an almost-constant basis. Since the mitzvah of rebuke is subject to the receiver's willingness to accept the responsible criticism, we are able to see that the purpose is solely for the spiritual well-being of the individual. Caring for others means trying to draw them closer to a Torah life that nourishes the soul, clarifies the doubts that vex so many of us, and enables growth.

VAYISHLACH

In this week's *parashah*, Yaakov is highly distraught over the questionable prospects of having a peaceful reunion with his brother Eisav. After many extensive preparations for possible conflict, they finally meet amicably and even embrace. During their exchange, Yaakov flatters Eisav by saying that his face is like the face of "*Elokim*." One has to wonder, "Why mention G-d? Why invoke that which drives them apart?" After all, it was the blessing of the Almighty that Yaakov would have dominion over Eisav. It seems dangerous to bring G-d into the conversation if Yaakov was really trying to do all he could to avoid antagonizing his brother.

Furthermore, there seems to be another misstep when Yaakov says, "*Ki chanani Elokim v'yesh li kol*," again referencing G-d's name and this time, seemingly, throwing it in Eisav's face that he has it all. Everything that the birthright blessing would have assured Eisav, the firstborn, came true for Yaakov. Why not keep the reunion conversation as short as possible so that Yaakov could safely journey on and establish his estate?

Perhaps, we could suggest that this would be the one opportunity that Yaakov would have to impart any influence over his brother in a way that would infuse a sense of G-dliness. This one encounter was the *only* chance to remind his brother of their upbringing and the values of their family. This message was dearer to Yaakov than any other possible objectives. He says, "*yesh li kol*" in order to show Eisav that the material blessings came true, and that one can have the pleasures of this world while simultaneously being with Hashem. Yaakov knew that Eisav was overcome with base desires, and now he could show him the largesse along with the Torah lifestyle that Eisav would otherwise never see. Yaakov's entire estate was in plain view, so he tried to use it to ignite something positive in Eisav.

When it comes to making Kiddush, the halachah is that a person can say Kiddush for a fellow Jew who has not yet heard it, even if he ends up saying it many times. (The same is true for other mitzvos as well.) Generally, we frown on making too many *berachos*. Are not these numerous recitations of Kiddush excessive? As the halachah indicates, we can say Kiddush multiple times because another Jew's obligation is also our personal obligation. We share the mitzvos, and due to our interconnectedness as a national family, someone else's obligation is also our own obligation. As long as another Jew has yet to be *mekadesh* Shabbos, my obligation, on some level, is incomplete, so I can say the *berachah* again despite my personal recitation already having taken place. This halachah allows us to see the concept of *areivus*; we are tied together as a people in a very tangible way.

Now we can know that, at the reunion with Eisav, Yaakov understood that he himself is incomplete and that his family is incomplete as long as Eisav has turned his back on leading a principled life. Yaakov knew he had to risk a precarious situation to try and light a spark of return for his brother. The Gemara teaches us that the ideal *chavrusah* is when two students challenge one another. Yaakov knew that no one other than he could help Eisav see the mistakes he was making. Out of a love for his brother, his parents, and his grandparents, he did all he could to share his Torah way of life. And, as Chazal tell us, at least the head of Eisav's body merited burial in *Me'aras Hamachpelah* (see *Sotah* 13b). May the Almighty help us remember our intimate connection as one big Jewish family so that we can look out for an even greater collective *avodas Hashem*.

VAYEISHEV

The *sidrah* tells us that Yosef's master, Potiphar, saw that Hashem was with Yosef. Potiphar himself was far removed from monotheism, so what exactly was he so easily able to recognize in Yosef? Was there a certain glow? What was different about Yosef in comparison to the rest of his servants?

Rashi tells us, *"shagur b'fiv,"* that Yosef's manner of speech revealed a Divine conscientiousness. The *Ramban*, however, disagrees and says that what struck Potiphar about Yosef was his actions. It was not Yosef's speech that stood out but rather that there seemed to be a providential watchguard over Yosef, evident in his unique accomplishments on behalf of Potiphar's enterprises.

This *sidrah* highlights an important lesson about the two kinds of reactions to success. One is to say, "Look what my Creator has helped me do," and the other is to say, "Look how talented I am." The first approach gives credit to Hashem, and the other says, *"Kochi v'otzem yadi asah li es ha'chayil ha'zeh."* Potiphar noticed that Yosef's handiwork caused his properties to flourish, but that Yosef lacked the ego that he would have expected him to have. (*Rashi* points out [39:11] that eventually Yosef disassociates just enough from this lofty level, and he, therefore, ends up in the scandal with Potiphar's wife, which led to his incarceration and the low point of his time in Egypt.)

Most impressively, Potiphar places Yosef as a supervisor, overseeing all of the other servants. This is quite striking, since the Egyptian people viewed the Hebrews as the lowest, most deplorable of all the nations in the world. Had Potiphar not realized the special *hashgachah* surrounding Yosef's actions, honoring Yosef in this fashion would have been unthinkable. Yosef was admired in this very way, and it was therefore passed down from Egyptian parent to child that Yosef exemplifies such a fine character that wondrously enabled those around him to prosper.

It is evident that these were the seeds planted by Hashem so that when the time came for the emancipation of the Jewish People many years later, Egyptian society could recall the seeds of their special relationship with the Almighty (41:16). There were many Jews who were hesitant to leave Mitzrayim as it was the only country they knew. In fact, during *yetzias Mitzrayim*, it was often the non-Jewish neighbors who prodded the Jews to leave. This is the meaning of the words of Rabban Gamliel in the Haggadah, "*Ki gurshu mi'Mitzrayim v'lo yachlu l'hismamehah*—because they were expelled from Egypt and could not tarry."

It is very easy in *galus* to lose sight of our identity and become detached from Torah habits and ideals. Perhaps, our best approach is to have the general population see us and say, "*ki Hashem ito...u'matzliach b'yado*," like Potiphar said about Yosef, implying that the Almighty is visible in how we conduct ourselves. One day soon, we too will be redeemed, and perhaps then our non-Jewish neighbors will encourage us to embrace our mantle of leadership regarding monotheistic Torah principles, so that we, as a unified people, may G-d willing yet fully embrace it ourselves!

MIKEITZ

Perhaps, the two most exemplary role models for coping with *galus* are Yosef and Mordechai. Both experienced Israel and the diaspora. Both were put in positions of power by their respective monarchies and given the vestments of power. Both were admired for their superior wisdom by societies that disdained the Jewish People. The Egyptian people would not eat any food that was touched by a Jew, and the Persians resented the ascendancy and the inclusion of the Jews within high society. How, then, was it possible for Yosef and Mordechai to rise within their societies?

Both Yosef and Mordechai were miraculously able to thrive despite such difficult circumstances because the general population saw their intellectual prowess. Pharaoh is shown Yosef's interpretation skills by his royal servant. Achashveirosh is similary shown Mordechai's loyalty and language skills as related to him by his royal attendant. Pharaoh says about Yosef, "*Ein navon v'chacham kamocha*," that no similar individual exists with a mind like his in all of the land. Amazingly, Pharoah describes this phenomenon with the words, "*Ish asher ruach Elokim bo*." Pharaoh, the world's leading pagan, sees the Divine spirit within Yosef.

Had Yosef preserved only his own spiritual life and his father's teachings, that would have been enough to impress. But we know that he was even able to impact those around him in a most difficult environment! He was able to save the Jewish People by situating them in Goshen. The fact that he was able to overcome all the temptations available to him as a beautiful, talented person is a credit to his determination to withstand the personal pressures of assimilation. When Yosef names his son Efraim, he acknowledges that he is in a precarious state and that the Almighty has helped him persevere. As it states, "*Ki hifrani Elokim b'eretz ani*—G-d has allowed me to flourish even in the land of my affliction."

Yosef and Mordechai shared their Divine knowledge with others. They did not do so by lecturing, but rather by becoming involved and contributing in a modest fashion. Yosef became the main advisor as it related to the famine, and Mordechai became a key advisor in Achasveirosh's court. The depth of their wisdom and the quality of their character were in plain sight for all to see and to acknowledge the Torah system that clearly inspired them. May the Almighty help us live with a dedication to Torah study so that, as we go through our daily routine, we too might be a living testament of the truth that enhances society and that brings those around us closer to Hashem.

VAYIGASH

As Yaakov comes to terms with the family needing to relocate to Mitzrayim because of the famine, we have a portal into how Jews are supposed to act in the diaspora. Upon his arrival, Yaakov meets with Pharaoh, the family represents Hashem to the Egyptian people, and they set up a community dedicated to learning. In order to prevent assimilation while living in this spiritually bereft environment for hundreds of years, certain practices were implemented as safeguards. As the midrash tells us, our ancestors maintained their ethnic clothing, Hebrew language, and their Jewish names. They even set up a yeshiva for all to witness how they spent their time wisely in Torah study. These specific elements of any given lifestyle will define what is broadcast to the outside world. The Jews in Mitzrayim did not just keep private rituals for themselves, rather they recognized that the way others viewed them and interacted with them would impact the way they viewed themselves. The Jewish Goshen townsmen thus had exceptionally important commercial relationships.

Despite being far from home, they purposely set up these barriers to reflect the obvious—that Am Yisrael is different. Undoubtedly, there were many Egyptian laws and practices that discriminated against the Jews. Keeping our own traditions of names, language, and dress allowed us to strengthen our commitment to our national mission. The goal to maintain our traditions in our difficult surroundings offered a concomitant opportunity—that we could be a positive influence on those around us in Egypt. And, in fact, our ability to impart monotheism had a profound impact on the populace. Perhaps, the greatest example of this is when Yaakov passed away, and the entire country mourned him deeply. The nation that had been most hated by Egypt had actually reached a point where they were celebrated, appreciated, and by extension, the Almighty could be praised by a people very distant from Torah.

Our daily acceptance of mitzvah living, the recitation of *Shema*, affirms our belief in one G-d uniquely connected to Klal Yisrael. Why don't we just say, "*Hashem Elokeinu, Hashem Echad*"? How do the words "*Shema Yisrael*" at the beginning of the verse enhance this thrice daily recitation? It is not enough to just believe that Hashem is the G-d of the Jewish People. The Jewish People need to be involved in understanding and living a life that reflects a Hashem reality. This is what the words "*Shema Yisrael*" mean. The *Rambam* says that if we cannot find a community of believers, then it is best to live secluded in a cave. Historically, though, none of our leaders have ever lived reclusively for those purposes. On the contrary, they all worked towards establishing societies that better reflect the values they wanted for their own families. In Western society today, it is known that being kind includes providing for the needy. After all, this comes straight out of our very own *Chumash*. However, what is less understood, yet equally important, is that the Jewish People need to stay committed to their own ideals. We cannot forsake who we are. *Shema Yisrael* means that our entire community needs to be seen as a people with a mission determined by the Almighty. Quite significantly, if globally we are seen as such by those around us, then we will treat ourselves and define ourselves as being worthy of admiration.

VAYECHI

When Yaakov passed away, the Torah specifies that he was mourned by the palace and by all the elder noblemen, as it states, *"kol avdei Pharaoh ziknei beiso v'chol ziknei eretz Mitzrayim."* Some of the *mefarshim* suggest that the surrounding countries sent their statesmen to the funeral procession. The *Seforno* (1475–1550) writes that they understood that if the highly educated Egyptians saw something powerful in Yaakov, then he must have special qualities to honor. The *Kli Yakar* (1550–1619) said that as soon as Yaakov died, the officials saw that the famine was returning in a very harsh way. Throughout the ages, many countries saw good tidings come along with the rise of the Jewish community. Many saw their countries take a turn for the worse when the reverse happened. The fact that the Egyptian officials at that time connected their fortunes to the Jewish leader was a remarkable turn of events.

Just like all their academics saw a direct correlation between the death of Yaakov and the downturn of the Egyptian people, so too it is a great *kiddush Hashem* when we, the descendants of Yaakov, help reveal the interconnectedness of nature and Torah. One prime example of this is the land of Israel. When the Jewish People do the mitzvos properly in the land of Israel, the fields sprout forth and provide plenty for the inhabitants. Conversely, when we don't behave properly, there is a harsh and destructive barrenness that wreaks discernible havoc. Perhaps, the origin of the natural world is the best example of this. Chazal teach us that the world was created for the sake of Torah (see also *Avos* 6:1). It should be given to the world through the Jewish People and Moshe; it should be studied and adhered to so that the world can continue to function.

We can suggest, based on the unique success during the famine, that the Egyptian people saw that if the world would have only been created to have a Yaakov Avinu and his family lead it, then that would have been enough. It was undeniable that Egypt was blessed because of Yaakov's presence and that there was a tangible notion of Divine providence. There are many different ways to spread the importance of Torah living, but, with further commitment, we can share our learning and our mitzvos so that we, the children of Israel, can continue the mission of bearing witness to the Almighty upon which Yaakov embarked.

SEFER SHEMOS

SHEMOS

As the generations in Egypt came and went, the fortunes of the Jewish People took a precipitous downturn. While their incomes went up, the anti-Semitism reached a crescendo. The *Kli Yakar* explains that the words in our *sidrah*, "*Va'yirbu va'yaatzmu b'meod meod*" mean there was great largesse, materially, for the Jewish People (the language is similar to the blessing of sustenance in the *Shema*, "*U'v'chol meodecha*"). Pharaoh felt it was necessary to tax and oppress the Jewish People before the nation became any stronger within Egypt.

The real struggle, though, was that the Jews themselves began to identify more with their wealth than with their ethics. We became susceptible to suspicion because we abandoned the lessons of Yaakov, Yosef, and the other Jewish leaders of that time. The *Kli Yakar* elaborates that when we read that "Yosef was no longer known," it means that Pharoah had trusted Yosef and his followers, but, since we no longer resembled that once scrupulous generation, he no longer recognized us as Yosef.

Lastly, the *Kli Yakar* explains that Egyptian leadership noticed the change in Jewish behavior. The words "*rav v'atzum mimenu*," that the Jews are too numerous for us, refers to our good deeds and our Torah. We were once known for our character. The decline in our behavior signaled that we were susceptible to a weakening of character and ethical living, so the Egyptian strategists schemed to further separate us from our traditional way of life. In fact, our demise began as we turned towards a more idolatrous lifestyle. As a consequence, the Egyptians began their new tax legislations for the pagan headquarters of their country.

The fate of the Jewish People is one fate. We are a small nation that is completely interconnected. If we do not help each other ensure a more inclusive, wholly committed Jewish community, our observance will collectively suffer. We will be less worthy of *hashgachah* and Hashem will see that His children, as a whole, are not worthy of redemption just like this *dor* in our *sidrah*. When we strengthen our belief and our fealty as one people, like the generation that left Mitzrayim, Hashem will reach out with "His strong hands" to gather us in, *b'meheirah v'yameinu*!

VA'EIRA

Why did Hashem need to use all these miracles to redeem the Jewish People? Why could Hashem not have used more natural means? Why not let Pharaoh just release us, since he did not want us there in the first place? The beginning of these answers is related to how the Jewish People fit in with the rest of the nations of the world. On the one hand, we are independent as a people, and, on the other hand, we have a unique responsibility to the rest of the world. This interconnectedness is part of how we ought to look at the *makkos* and the related *nissim*.

At the beginning of the *parashah*, Hashem reaffirms the commitment of giving the land of Canaan to the Jewish People. Why was the smallest of lands promised to our matriarchs and patriarchs? Wouldn't the Torah have a bigger influence on society if we had one of the larger countries? Our *sidrah* provides great insight when reading the words, "*Baavur haroscha es kochi u'lemaan saper shimcha b'chol ha'aretz.*" All events were orchestrated not just for Jewish liberation but also in order that Hashem could show Pharaoh His power, spreading the name of G-d throughout the world. If there would have been no pomp along with the Exodus, then the Jewish People would not have been able to accomplish spreading the word about the Almighty's dominion. Moshe himself remarks to Pharaoh, "*Yadati ki terem tirun mi'pnei Hashem,*" implying that the Jewish People will not leave before Egypt knows the extent of G-d's prowess. Hashem says to Moshe explicitly that the *makkos* need to result in awareness of the Almighty and only then, "*V'hotzeisi es b'nei Yisrael mi'tocham,*" the Jewish People will be brought out. The *Netziv* further clarifies that "brought out" also means a spiritual rehabilitation from all the psychological and theological harm done to them as slaves.

As this week's portion indicates, the existence of the Jewish People is tied to proper Torah awareness by those around us. First, we need to know ourselves who we are and what we are meant to accomplish. Then, as that recognition improves, the world will come to a better understanding of the Almighty. Just like the miracles were necessary as part of the lesson of G-d for the nations of the world, which certainly impacts us as well, so too the smallness of Israel makes it even more extraordinary and even more miraculous that we can have such a deep impact on the world. By working toward these ends, we can begin to heal from this long and painful *galus*. Through sharing our tradition with our brothers and sisters, we can work more effectively to be an *or la'goyim* (*Yeshayahu* 49:6).

BO

The *Korban Pesach* was a turning point for our ancestors (*Ramban*, 12:3). The ability to *shecht* the lamb, which was deified by Egypt, gave them the confidence that they could embark on their journey as told to them by their ancestors throughout the generations. While they knew about the promise of living in Israel, witnessing this sacrifice made it real. The *dor ha'midbar* needed this boost to carry them through the wilderness as proven by their *emunah* deficiencies that led them to worship the golden calf. They were very close to completely assimilating and needed to stake out their identity. In fact, of the three million ancestral refugees, many were otherwise religiously comparable to the same Egyptian idolatrous soldiers that drowned, but the Jews at least had the *Korban Pesach* to boost their worthiness.

The *Ramban* explains that the visual impact of seeing their slaveholders' god slaughtered woke them up to the possibilities for their future. This act of the *Am Ha'nivchar* facilitating Hashem's victory over idolatry was a prerequisite for *yetzias Mitzrayim*. Moreover, the timing of leaving Egypt in the springtime was, in part, motivated by the Egyptian zodiac calendar. Chazal explain that the message was amplified because it was precisely at this time of year that the Egyptians looked to their gods to ensure their agricultural well-being (*Aruch Hashulchan* 429).

In many ways, Judaism can be summed up as Torah versus idolatry. Our motives are either pure with G-dly intentions or impure with ulterior intentions. The act of remembering what took place in Mitzrayim is one of the 613 commandments. What greater fulfillment of *zecher* could there be than, along with verbalizing the memory, that we consider what inspired actions can be taken in our own diaspora to wake ourselves up to our uniqueness. We may not be able to *shecht* an idol, but we can certainly work on a broader scale to identify what is foreign within our religiosity and what is authentic.

We have many debates as to what ought to be included in our Torah lifestyles, but we can all agree that educating ourselves through learning can help us understand the world and our Creator. May the Almighty preserve us, prevent our assimilation, and give us the strength to turn away from falsehood like our ancestors did. By actively participating in a more inclusive Torah educational experience defined by reaching out to others, then a more achievable clarity of Klal Yisrael's mission and purpose can be clinched!

BESHALACH

In our *sidrah*, Moshe and Yehoshua collaborate to select soldiers for the Jewish People. With this episode, we get great insight into how to become Moshe-approved defenders of Am Yisrael, even for today. As understood throughout the millennia, the war against Amalek is an ongoing one, where we always have to be vigilant. Rav Yaakov Moshe Charlop explained that this war is not really against an enemy nation as much as it is against the threat of a dangerous ideology. Amalek sought to have human behavior determined by whatever value system man selected for himself. In other words, they sought a world where there was no objective right and wrong. Everything was in the realm of *reshus*. So, Rav Charlop explained that the obligation for us throughout the ages is to teach the concept of living a life of principle. We need to learn from our *sidrah* how to exemplify ethical living through a decision-making process facilitated by Torah.

The *Ramban* explains that the *kisei ha'kavod* (throne of glory) will always be in conflict with the damaging values of the Amalekim. Furthermore, he says that the word "throne" is deliberately written without the *aleph* at the end—as "*keis*" instead of "*kisei*" at the very end of the *sidrah*—to teach us that it is up to Klal Yisrael to recognize that Hashem's kingdom is not complete so long as we are not protecting Torah from the onslaught of foreign philosophies like those of Amalek.

When Moshe requests that Yehoshua recruit for this conflict, he says to recruit *anashim* (men), which appears to be an extraneous detail, according to *Rashi*, thus alluding to a meaningful lesson. The *Maharal* (1520–1609) deduces that Chazal are trying to tell us that Moshe and Yehoshua were looking for the ranks to be filled by individuals who were particularly in awe of Heaven. Historically, most armies of the world throw the lower classes to the frontlines to serve as human fodder in armed conflicts. The Jewish People are different in that we look to our most pious to represent us on the battlefield, knowing well that our successful outcomes are dependent upon our worthiness and the Divine providence that inspects our character. Our mitzvah-oriented mentality is our best defense in the struggles against Amalek.

The mitzvos of remembering and of destroying Amalek are equally applicable today. While citizens of Amalek might not be easily recognizable today, in recent centuries it has certainly become more about the threat to a Torah way of life than the physical fight. For people who have been privileged to live closely connected to our tradition, it is incumbent upon us to be a part of the *milchemes Hashem* and the effort to share our rich way of life with other Jews so that they do not get swallowed up by the allure of that which is antithetical to our *mesorah*. Our families should not take who we are for granted, and we should celebrate more broadly the great opportunity of being ambassadors for Torah living.

YISRO

At the beginning of our *sidrah*, we are told that Yisro heard "all" that had transpired throughout the journey of Am Yisrael. Surely, if Yisro showed up, he must have been very impressed. We are told by our Sages that Yisro was very taken with the theology of Torah, and was impressed enough to withstand the backlash from his neighbors for embracing the leader of the Hebrews as a son-in-law (*Sotah* 11a). A few verses later, we read, "*Va'yesaper Moshe l'chosno*," that Moshe told Yisro all that took place. In both sentences when we are told "He [i.e., Yisro] heard" and that "Moshe told" him, it states explicitly, "*Eis kol asher asah Hashem*," that all events were reviewed again directly by Moshe to Yisro. If Yisro already knew this, as the Torah states, then why did Moshe have to go over it again, or at least he could delegate this historical review of an already familiar account? In addition, why not just let the family reunion take place, and let Yisro take a load off after his long journey?

The answer is that Moshe wasn't going to let a moment go to waste without praising the Almighty's wondrous acts on behalf of the survival of the Jewish People. He certainly wasn't going to delegate this menial task to others, and their recent history was critical to share with all those who entered the camp, so they knew what *machaneh Yisrael* was all about. Sure, Moshe could have had a *shaliach* teach the details and maybe even invoked a stratagem of *shlucho shel adam k'moso*, but the opportunity was much too dear to pass the responsibility on to someone else. After all, his father-in-law was a man of great prestige on the international stage, and conveying this message directly to him was the equivalent of influencing many different nations, based on him being well-known among the nations of the world.

We see that Moshe's "current events lesson" had an impact, because it states immediately thereafter that Yisro rejoiced over "*kol ha'tovah asher asah Hashem l'Yisrael*," which means for all the goodness wrought by the Almighty for Klal Yisrael. The harsh reality, though, is that redemption only occurred to, and was able to free, just twenty percent of the entire nation. Many did not make it to see all the *nissim* and *niflaos* performed on our behalf.

The *Netziv* explains that Moshe elucidated the full extent of what happened with all the particulars. Yisro knew generally what happened, but that wasn't enough for Moshe. Besides the number of miracles, many of which are referenced in the Haggadah, Moshe taught Yisro that it was specifically done to publicize the intellectual truths of Hashem's dominion and subjugation of the mighty Egyptian empire. Moshe wanted to convey that the emancipation was secondary, and the Jewish People as a vehicle for broadcasting monotheism was primary.

One might think that G-d using us for His own publicist purposes is degrading, but rather, on the contrary, Moshe is teaching Yisro and the rest of us that it is the highest honor. Our freedom was not free per se, but rather comes with a unique, direct mission. One way to look at it is that the Kohen Gadol might be seen as the most prominent and powerful Jew in our ranks, yet has the most regimented, strict life of all the citizenry. His efforts might decide the determination of atonement on Yom Kippur or the assessment of going out to war, however, the Kohen Gadol is a vehicle for *avodah* (service).

May the Almighty give us the clarity of mind and purpose to embrace the prestige of being a tool of expression for the ideals of the Torah. And may we too be worthy of having a *geulah b'karov* with a renewed appreciation from our *parashah* of following in Moshe's footsteps by personally involving ourselves in expressing to others the miraculous journey of the Jewish People.

MISHPATIM

There is often a debate as to whether it's better to actively engage a matter that is abhorrent or to ignore it altogether so as to not validate it. Our *sidrah* takes a clear stance that idolatrous philosophies need to be acted against forcefully. The *Chumash* is discussing an angel of Hashem, referred to as a defender of Klal Yisrael, that will protect it from its enemies. Therefore, the Torah goes out of its way to reissue and reiterate the command to proactively avoid worship of other gods. The Torah goes a step further, however, and commands us to rid ourselves of false deities. Therefore, we have two commandments reinforcing this notion: one listed among the negative mitzvos, and also one listed among the positive mitzvos more generally of belief. Let us turn our attention to these two examples: Thou shalt not worship and Thou shalt destroy these gods.

The *Kli Yakar* further explains that there is unique reward for fulfilling these commandments. If we pay close attention, we'll see that the reward for sincerely serving the Almighty is written in the singular "*U'veirach es lachmecha v'es meimecha*," that your bread (food) and water (drink) will be blessed plentifully, while the word "*Va'avaditem es Hashem*," "that you'll worship the Almighty" is written in the plural. This incongruity was written intentionally to teach us the extent to which we rely on one another. The *Kli Yakar* explains that these words underscore "*kol Yisrael areivim zeh ba'zeh*," which means that just because people might personally serve G-d well in their own private homes, that does not mean that there will be reward. Only when mitzvah observance is collectively and communally at a high level will the *berachos* referenced in this week's portion come to fruition. Unity isn't just a nice idea but rather indispensable.

Lastly, the *Seforno* elucidates that one might think that serving G-d is somewhat of a separate effort from fighting the encroachment of the many enticing false theologies around us. Rather, the *Seforno* says the precise way to show service to G-d is to undermine the grasp of that which is antithetical to Torah. In that way, we'll allow our people to flourish, and we'll fulfill all the related commandments surrounding appropriate religious piety. These ideas are prominently highlighted within the first of the *Aseres Hadibros* as well.

Many times, in our communities, we see only what's in front of us, failing to take note of the breadth of world Jewry that is not in our vicinity. We often presume that we are free from tackling issues of Jewish illiteracy and assimilation, which have been fostered in part due to the proliferation of influential falsehoods, because it doesn't impact us directly or it's too big of an issue for us to solve. By looking at this week's comments from the *Seforno* and the *Kli Yakar*, we can ask Hashem to help us take heart in staying true to our commitment to preserving Torah beyond our immediate circles.

TERUMAH

When comparing and contrasting the *Mishkan*, *Bayis Rishon*, and *Bayis Sheini*, one could point to a number of discrepancies between them. One example includes the collection of gifts gathered from Am Yisrael for the purposes of constructing the *Mishkan* (Tabernacle). As we'll see below, the sources of donations differ between these three houses of Hashem. The commanding verse issues a proclamation to "B'nei Yisrael," and then reiterates "*Me'eis* ***kol*** *ish asher yidvenu libo*," meaning it first references the Jewish People then states "all" who are moved to contribute. The *Beis Haleivi* (1820–1892) finds a deeply meaningful message within this one phrase emphasizing inclusion. The additional expectation of everyone giving is said to encourage the acceptance of the philanthropy of the *eiruv rav*. The *eiruv rav* are understood to be the Jews who lived within the *dor ha'midbar* and did not believe in G-d or our system of mitzvos (*Rashi*, 34:1). Astoundingly, Hashem goes out of the way to make sure that the gifts of these fringe elements were part of the nation's spiritual headquarters. Our *pasuk* goes out of the way to teach us this *din* because we would have presumed an invalid status would be the label for all the gifts from those who held on to aspects of their previous anti-monotheist beliefs. It's also particularly remarkable when considering that this generation witnessed the greatest the miracles in world history, and yet still had heretics living in their midst.

This ethic is reinforced by Chazal in the opening teaching from the fourth chapter of the Mishnah in *Avos*. Ben Zoma advises that a wise man is defined as one who is able to learn from all humanity. Honor of the Almighty is the goal (*Avos* 6:11). Many struggle with lowering themselves to be students of "lesser" instructors, but when they realize that learning is for the sake of the Almighty, and not their own honor, then their ability to humble themselves becomes greater. Just like the *Mishkan* was built by all the masses, so too our community needs to be built up with the uplifting purity of diversity as identified in our *sidrah*. Broadening the tent and reaching out to all kinds of Jews are two of the critical strategies for increasing *kedushah* within our *kehillos*. Just as the original *kedushah* of the *Mikdash* was set up with extensively varied contributors, so too there's a lesson here for us that a prerequisite for *ruchniyus* is nonconformity, in the sense that the *Mishkan* and the *kehillah* Ben Zoma wants us to have means encouraging diversity of opinion.

Rav Shimon Schwab asks why *nedavos* were taken only from Jews for the *Mishkan* and *Bayis Sheini*, but non-Jews were able to help Shlomo HaMelech construct *Bayis Rishon*. Rav Schwab answers that Shlomo correctly predicted that, unlike the other houses of Hashem, *Bayis Rishon* would be a focal point for the entire world. People from all over the earth would travel to Yerushalayim to quench their thirst for Torah knowledge (*Melachim I*, chap. 5). Therefore, their sincere financial assistance was ruled to be suitable for use in the construction of the Beis Hamikdash. On the other hand, non-Jews were never so moved to frequent the *Mishkan* or *Bayis Sheini* en masse, so such approval would be disingenuous. Naturally, all Jews benefit from the capital of the Torah world and thus need to be able to find their place to be a part of our national mission. The messages of the *Beis Haleivi* and Rav Schwab have been lost over the years of internal bickering between rival Jewish factions. To fulfill the imperative, "*V'asu li Mikdash v'shachanti b'socham*," we'd be best served to recall these measures of unity necessary for creating the eternal third Beis Hamikdash, may it come quickly in our days, *b'meheirah b'yameinu*.

TETZAVEH

Much of this week's *sidrah* is a summary of the various responsibilities of Aharon and the Kohanim. After the sin of the *egel ha'zahav,* the Kohanim took over from the firstborn the role of serving in the *Mishkan*. The firstborns were complicit in leading the disastrous episode of the golden calf and, therefore, lost their privileges. The Kohanim were thus consecrated to Hashem to perform the *avodah*. The first of every womb, both man and animal, are similarly consecrated as well.

The *Kli Yakar* teaches us the uniqueness of Aharon when describing in *Vayikra* why Aharon and his descendants were designated to be the authority on *nega'im*. The commentary states that Aharon was primarily defined by his pursuit of peace within Klal Yisrael, his unique, extraordinary humility, and his lack of interest in materialism. This is also why Hillel exhorts us, in the first *perek* in *Avos*, to be among the disciples of Aharon. The culmination of this life lesson is "*oheiv es ha'briyos u'mekarvan la'Torah,*" which means to love people and to draw them close to Torah. There are many commentaries that capture the full intent of this teaching. Suffice it to say that if one is committed to enhancing feelings of kinship throughout Hashem's world, then part of that process is sharing Torah in an inspiring manner. The *mefarshim* explain that Aharon disregarded any fear of befriending and being influenced by the wrong crowd. Aharon understood the great powers of clarity that learning Torah brings into what can otherwise be a very confusing life journey. He greatly believed in Torah, and he loved others enough that failing to share the truths of Torah would be unconscionable.

Aharon was attuned to the notion that, left unchecked, the *yetzer hara* (evil inclination) will overpower man. In Hashem's great mercy, He gave us the Torah as a *tavlin*, an antidote to the incredible power of the evil inclination. Aharon was also abiding by the commandment of "*Lo saamod al dam rei'echa.*" This mitzvah, which requires us to not stand idly by our fellow's demise, is also understood as applying to our neighbor's spiritual well-being. Aharon understood that the spiritual essence of another was included just like the physical condition.

Maybe we would have thought that the group responsible for *kedushas Yisrael* ought to distance themselves from the *sheker* of those far removed from a life of Torah and mitzvos, but our *sidrah* teaches us that it is precisely those set aside for administrating the *makom haShechinah* who are positioned to draw the entirety of the Jewish community closer to Hashem. Indeed, the descendants of Aharon, who uniquely understood the equal importance of the man-man relationship commandments and the man-Hashem related commandments, were particularly well appointed for these tasks. As we seek to be more deserving of the title *Am Kadosh*, may the Almighty grant us the strength to lovingly share the Torah's wisdom that provides so many restorative answers to life's most challenging issues.

KI SISA

In our *sidrah*, we read the famous words, "*V'shamru v'nei Yisrael es haShabbos*," and there are already many other instances in which the Jewish People are commanded to observe Shabbos and keep the day of rest as sacrosanct. The *Ohr Hachaim* (1696–1743) understands these words written in the plural as being a demand on Klal Yisrael as a collective to keep the Shabbos from being desecrated. He rightly predicted with his profound vision that there would be those who incorrectly relate to Shabbos as he writes, "*V'lo yomar adam dai li ba'meh she'nishmor atzmo mei'chalalo v'im yischalel mei'ha'zoles mah b'kach*"—That a person shouldn't say, 'It's enough for me to observe Shabbos, and what is it to me that someone else should desecrate Shabbos.'" Alas, many of us have such a relationship with Shabbos and thus fail to live up to the mitzvah of *shemiras Shabbos* accordingly. Whether or not we ought to consider ourselves *shomer Shabbos*, if we do or do not work on behalf of the dignity of Shabbos is a discussion for another instance. But it's sufficient for our purposes to say that this famous *pasuk* recited weekly ought to inspire us toward learning more about Shabbos. The *Ohr Hachaim* continues saying that as a foundational element of *Yahadus* and the symbol of the relationship we have with the Almighty, our avoidance of creative labor is not simply the avoidance of transgressing negative commandments but is an active fulfillment of positive commandments, as we proactively create an atmosphere ripe for *kedushah*.

This fundamental mitzvah is not the only mitzvah in our *sidrah*. As the Jewish People erred with the *eigel ha'zahav*, our commentaries teach us that unlike all other idolatrous activity, the Jewish People didn't actually believe that the golden calf had any powers over and outside the purview of the Almighty (*Shemos Rabbah*). That said, as a nation charged with the responsibility of spreading the message of Torah, the error was so egregious that Hashem wanted to destroy Am Yisrael, and Moshe had to smash the *luchos* in order to save our future (*Rashi, Devarim* 34:12). The *Ramban* explains that the three most famous words of our portion, "*Mi la'Hashem eilai*," were yelled by Moshe at the gate of the camp in a very dramatic fashion, because he recognized that the grave consequences of Klal Yisrael spiritually pivoting away from the Ribbono Shel Olam would lead to absolute derision from the nations of the world and would mean the end of the global mission to bring the world toward a mindfulness of G-d. Moshe was aware that very little could be accomplished by just the efforts of a small fraction of Jewry, and that an overhaul through *teshuvah* would be necessary to clinch our national righteous ambitions. We should see this as foreshadowing that there will be times when the Jewish People will become complacent and forget that observance needs to be fostered more widely.

This moral truism is reflected in the nothingness of individual man as taught with the words "*mah ani*" in *Pirkei Avos*. Hillel famously stated, "If I am for myself, then what am I?" In other words, if a Jew, or, as in Moshe's understanding, even a small number of Jews, were to exist alone, then what value would we have? A Jew needs to take responsibility for his fellow Jews. This is true for our theological keystones like Shabbos and idolatry, but it is certainly representative of Torah as a whole. If *talmud Torah* and our general *mesorah* is not shared with those Jews who are more distant from it, then it is the "broader-we" who are lacking in quality. May the Almighty give us the insight to internalize the meaning of *v'shamru*, written in the plural, and to echo the rallying call of Moshe Rabbeinu in this week's *sidrah* of *Mi la'Hashem eilai*!

VAYAKHEL-PEKUDEI

As the team of builders got together to formally begin construction of the *Mishkan*, we should note the requirements necessary to participate with Betzalel, the lead builder. The verse states, "*V'chol chacham lev bachem yavo'u v'yaasu*," which means all hearts of wisdom among the nation were welcome to labor for the *Mishkan*. The *Netziv* notes the word "*v'chol*" as uniquely inviting those who lack expertise in Torah knowledge. "*Chacham lev*" was essentially a euphemism for those who feared the Almighty yet had no other qualities. Their *lev*, or heart, was in the right place, but they had no prowess in other areas. The commentary continues that word would be sent out to those who didn't study the word of G-d. They were *amei ha'aretz*, as we might refer to them today, and completely ignorant of any of the background of Hashem's laws. Moreover, they brought zero artisan skills to the process, and they also did not have any professional training from the old country, Egypt. Too often, we ask for so many qualifications and for so many proverbial boxes to be checked that we forget the main criteria is sincerity.

This message of inclusivity is furthered by Rav Yaakov Kamenetsky when pointing out that the words in the *sidrah*'s opening verse contrast strongly with the Har Sinai experience. Famously, the Sages teach us that "*Vayichan sham Yisrael neged ha'har*" is written in the singular to teach us that the Jewish People were unified, like one man with one heart, when they encamped altogether, wholly committed to the goals of a Jewish destiny defined by Torah living. In our *sidrah*, however, work was needed to bring us back to that point as a people. As such, our weekly portion begins, "*Vayakhel Moshe es kol adas B'nei Yisrael.*" In the aftermath of Hashem's forgiveness and the receiving of the second *luchos*, Moshe strives to unite the people as he gathers the entire *adas* (flock). As they prepare for the Divine residence in the *Mishkan*, they needed to come together as one big Jewish family. Rav Kamenetsky explained that, at this moment, there was a lot of finger pointing and blaming between the different tribes for what caused the incident with the golden calf. On some level, we could proffer that the potency of diverse Jewish togetherness has the ability to "bring down" the *Shechinah* upon Earth. Indeed, as the people of the book, chosen by the Almighty, we are meant to mimic the oneness of Hashem by powerfully repairing our fractures for the sake of our own oneness.

As Chazal extraordinarily detail for us, David HaMelech's generation had much Torah but little peace because of their disjointed nature and their mistreatment of each other. This is in contradistinction to the *achdus* that Klal Yisrael had during the times of Achav HaMelech, when they were living lives that were not only not in accordance with the Torah but were outright antithetical to Torah. The power of reaching out to one another and having a cohesive Am Yisrael cannot be overstated enough. We need everyone regardless of his level of Torah observance and for tolerance to reign over certain cracks in our ranks in order to again experience a more tangible *v'shachanti b'socham*, the Almighty in our midst.

SEFER VAYIKRA

VAYIKRA

The end of our *sidrah* discusses returning lost objects to their rightful owners and the requirement to pay restitution when financially wronging one's neighbor. The responsibility of making another financially whole is part of creating a just and ethical society. The way the Almighty made the world lends itself to more easily understanding returning an object relative to returning a spiritual sense of well-being. *Teshuvah* (repentance) is linguistically connected to a concept of returning, albeit in this context it refers to returning to one's ideal self and to one's Creator.

Indeed, the Chafetz Chaim's *Chomas Hadaas* draws heavily on these ideas when imploring his generation to heed the lessons of *baalei teshuvah*. Secularism was wreaking havoc on the populace around Poland, and the Chafetz Chaim wanted to teach the community that while it's obligatory to return property to a fellow Jew, it is even more significant to return the Jewish heritage to our fellow Jews. While physical poverty and its devastating impact is easily perceivable, spiritual poverty (i.e., a distancing between a Jew and Torah), which can be imperceptible, is much more destructive. After all, Chazal tell us that while parents physically give life, teachers of Torah provide spiritual life. If we saw someone drowning, would we not do everything in our power to try and save the person? The Chafetz Chaim asks that we give the same level of import as we would to saving someone from drowning to preserving the Torah tradition for as many Jews as possible. The *Yerushalmi* rules that we are obligated to even put ourselves in a position of potential peril for lifesaving purposes. When considering individually and collectively how to proceed with strengthening diaspora Jewry, we ought to make sure that we aren't overly risk averse. Relatedly, Rav Yaakov Kamenetsky taught his students that there's a *havtachah* (assurance) that if one takes care of the Almighty's children, then the Almighty will take care of one's children. If we believe in the truth and power of the Almighty's Torah, then how can we not redouble our efforts to reach out to Am Yisrael.

It is no wonder that our *sidrah* juxtaposes returning lost items and the concept of *shogeig* (violation due to lack of awareness). The referenced atonement offering, according to the Gemara, corresponds to the error of being unaware. The obligation to make up an unjust financial loss caused to someone often arises due to a person's haphazard, careless approach to his fellow's property. The Torah requires us to be responsible and thoughtful about our fellow man and requires us to be on guard at all times from causing harm to another or his property.

Moreover, in this week's commentary of the *Ramban*, when discussing the role of the atonement *korban*, the *Ramban* suggests a more expansive view of who constitutes community. The *Ramban* further describes the etymology of "***korban***" by underscoring how "offering" is related to "***karov***," and how the institution of *avodah* is meant to draw all members of the congregation "closer" to Hashem. This is not a personal agenda but, as described, is certainly a national agenda for which we are each responsible. The *Kli Yakar* describes how there are two instances of *shogeig* or ignorant acts: a person who is educated and acts absentmindedly, and a person who lacks awareness because he never learned about such a thing. The sages tell us that with knowledge comes responsibility, thereby making the absentmindedness more culpable. This leads us to the *Kli Yakar*'s comments later in the *sidrah* that places the highest level of blame on the Kohen Gadol and the halachic authorities. By extension, one can naturally conclude that the Torah communities on a broader, collective scale bear the burden of the most weight for the community's fulfillment of mitzvos. May the Almighty grant us the ability to restore our connection to one another and return en masse with a great *teshuvah* soon in our days!

TZAV

When we contemplate the glory years of the Jewish People, our imagination is often captured by the *Urim V'Tumim* (the breastplate with twelve stones worn by the Kohen Gadol). We recall with amazement how all of Am Yisrael lived together in tranquility under Shlomo HaMelech, and whenever a national emergency arose, they consulted the *Urim V'Tumim*, and the Almighty would respond with clear direction. The resulting blessing of clarity and the ensuing peace of mind was arguably the greatest blessing of all.

When contemplating why *Bayis Rishon* had this revered *choshen* and *Bayis Sheini* did not, we ought to conclude in part that the reason is due to the fracturing of our people. (*Rashi* explains that the *choshen* existed, but that Hashem's name was missing from inside the breastplate, thereby rendering it inoperable.) After all, there were upon it twelve stones corresponding to the twelve tribes, with the names of each etched therein. But the connections between the *Shevatim* were severed at the time of the second Beis Hamikdash. A reasonable strategy for returning the miracle of the *Urim V'Tumim* would be to clinch the unity that it requires. Then our national sense of direction will improve, and issues of faith would cease. One could suggest further that the breastplate was worn by Aharon and not Moshe, because Aharon is identified as the leader who reinstated *shalom* between quarrelsome rivals. Indeed, Moshe lost the honor to be in Aharon's position because he forwent the opportunity to unite the Jewish People under his leadership. His hesitation resulted in passing that privilege to Aharon. Additionally, Chazal tell us that this special *choshen* was there to make amends for national issues of justice that threatened to divide our people. The sages further tell us that the *Urim V'Tumim* is representative of ideal brotherhood. When Moshe saw Aharon with this special royal garb and the awesome powers that came with it, he was genuinely happy that his brother had this historic honor. Similarly, Aharon's feelings for Moshe are underscored here as well. Aharon's worldview highlighted that a person need not see his neighbor as a rival. Aharon challenged the philosophy that there are a finite number of assets in the world, and if my friend has something precious, then I cannot have it. In other words, *l'havdil*, just because the person next door has a luxury convertible doesn't mean that I cannot have it. Each of us has enough independence that we have our own realities. Aharon saw the ascension of Moshe, his only brother, not as a threat but as a source of pride that someone so close to him could reach such lofty levels of accomplishment.

When reading this week of Aharon's merits and the famous *Urim V'Tumin*, let us consider the message of a broader harmony without conformity. In other words, all the stones were distinct, yet powerfully connected. We all have ways in which we are dissimilar, but we need to sincerely stand up for one another and to take responsibility for our interconnected, higher well-being. We need to reach out beyond our own immediate circles in spreading Torah so that we can achieve a single-mindedness of G-d conscientiousness that will assuredly lead to the reinstallation of the *choshen* and its peacefulness once again for all of Klal Yisrael.

SHEMINI

Our *sidrah* goes into great detail regarding the prominence of the *Mizbei'ach*, which is one of Aharon's caretaking responsibilities and correspondingly one of the most significant activities of the Kohanim. The *Kli Yakar* explains that the relationship between Aharon and the *Mizbei'ach* could be characterized by the words in the *pasuk*, "*Vechaper baadcha u'v'ad ha'am*," which means that the atonement for Aharon personally and the atonement collectively for the Jewish People were linked together. If Aharon couldn't facilitate the national penitence, then he would personally be held accountable. Markedly, the midrash relays these sentiments when describing why in our *sidrah* Moshe and Aharon go into the inner chamber, otherwise known as the *Ohel Mo'ed* of the *Mishkan*. The stakes were very high, and Moshe helped Aharon with the required *ketores* component of the *avodah* (*Rashi*, *Bamidbar* 17:9). Moshe needed to perform an intervention specifically in light of the fatal error of Nadav and Avihu, the attending Kohanim and the children of Aharon. The officiant would be held responsible for any mistakes.

The *Ohr Hachaim* relays the tradition that Nadav and Avihu had good intentions and would not have been so severely punished had it not been for their high-stakes responsibility for each individual. The end of our *sidrah* provides additional reinforcement when noting the Torah's emphasis of the Almighty's holiness and our related holiness meant to fulfill an agenda of *kedushah*. It stands to reason that those who are in a position where so much is expected of them are held to a higher standard (*Sanhedrin* 8a). Those of us privileged to learn and to live a life of Torah will be accountable for our national prospects.

Lastly, the *Seforno* elucidates the phrase of *Ohel Mo'ed* via the term and the category of *mo'adim*. Whereas the tent of meeting was a place of intimate connection to the Almighty, so too the days on the calendar, referred to as the holidays or the *mo'adim*, are days of intimate connection with the Ribbono Shel Olam. As we go into our family holiday experiences, we should bear in mind the lessons of our *sidrah*. We should recall the words of the *Rambam* and *Rashi* that the obligation of having joy on the festivals, as required by the Torah, includes an added effort to reach out to our fellow Jews to make sure that they are partaking in the celebrations. *Rashi* (*Devarim* 16:11) comments that helping others experience *simchah* on Yom Tov will assure our households of experiencing *simchah* on Yom Tov and beyond. The *Rambam*'s description underscores that being stuck with an inward focus is in contradiction to the *mo'adim*, as people due to monetary issues or other circumstances beyond their control won't have a Yom Tov experience without help. The *Rambam* continues that it is detestable to G-d for a person to lock his gates and feed his family while leaving those on the outside looking in. Just like there are those who have financially fallen behind, so too there are those who have spiritually fallen behind. Looking at this law with more scrutiny allows us to better appreciate the psychological truths therein. Celebrating by oneself is not enjoyable when compared to sharing in jubilation with those less religiously or economically fortunate in our community. The Jewish People are uniquely linked together as one big family inside the House of Yaakov, as seen through the processes surrounding the *Mizbe'ach* and the *Ohel Mo'ed*. May Hashem bless our households with success as we endeavor to connect Am Yisrael with a special closeness to Hakadosh Baruch Hu!

TAZRIA-METZORA

When considering the disease of *tzaraas*, we see it as an affliction without parallel. It is a supernatural gift from the Almighty to have an indicator that one's life has gone awry and corrective measures need to be taken to get back on track. One of the seven *aveiros* (and the first *aveirah* listed in the Gemara) that results in *tzaraas* is *lashon hora*. Considering all the terrible ramifications of *lashon hara*, it is fortunate to be told that a person erred so that he could fix his mistake. One's physiological health would be threatened if he didn't have the ability to feel heat or pain. The same is true spiritually. If one can't sense what's impacting him, then he can't avoid the source of his ailment. *Tzaraas*, which is often poorly translated as leprosy, forces us to pause to take a timeout to collect ourselves and reconcile with those we've crossed. Due to the erosion of our worthiness, we no longer have the *tzaraas* warning system. However, it is axiomatic that the more worthy we collectively become, then the more likely we will be rewarded with the higher spiritual levels and opportunities that defined our existence.

Sometimes, the best defense is a good offense. The way to avoid pitfalls of ill-speech perpetrated against one's fellow man is to better understand them. The *Yerushalmi* tells us that just like a kitchen mishap in which the right hand accidentally wounds the left hand would never result in the left hand exacting revenge on the right hand, so too a Jew, who properly perceives the Jewish People as one, could never attack his Jewish brother or sister. There is a common history and common bond forged through the eternality of Torah that makes such a possible sinful act completely nonsensical. Just like gossip uniquely fractures a community, so too does the failure to effectively unite others with *harbatzas Torah* (the spreading of Torah). Only a maniac would allow one hand to cut his other hand to make it fair, and the same is true when concerning another Jew or group of Jews.

The complicating factor is that, if we do not reach out one to the other in a spirit of Torah, we will naturally be estranged from each other. How can we not see ourselves as disparate groups if we don't take the Torah that binds us to connect our disconnected sub-groups? It's easier to speak poorly of people who are unfamiliar, and it's more difficult to do so if we are all residing in the same proverbial *beis midrash*. The fact that *lashon hora* and not Shabbos or kashrus or many other possible examples lead to this extraordinary skin ailment, perhaps should give us pause to reflect how much the Almighty wants us to be joined together as one. *Lashon hara*, as a negative, teaches us to view ourselves as equals. Indeed, the ultimate *geulah* during *yetzias Mitzrayim* is said to have been experienced by the one *dor* known to have been compliant with the rules of *lashon hora*. The Chafetz Chaim quotes our sages as saying that redemption could not have been possible had they not been obeying these laws of speech. Indeed, the Almighty tells us that, "if you can't even speak nicely about each other, then I don't want to be with you." As Mar Ukva says in the Gemara, based on a *pasuk* in *Tehillim*, "With regard to anyone who speaks malicious speech, the Holy One, blessed be He, says about him: He and I cannot dwell together in the world."

There's a certain heresy that exists when one maligns another, as if we are not all a part of the same body. There's an implicit denial of all that we've been through together throughout history and all that we have yet to accomplish as per our future that's been foretold by the *neviim*. May the Almighty grant us the strength to reach out to each other, regardless of our demographics, with interactions infused with Torah so that our speech and behavior lead us back to a rebuilt promised land as it did so many generations ago!

ACHAREI MOS

In our *sidrah*, we discuss the processional of the *seirim* and the process through which Klal Yisrael receive atonement. When talking about the day of atonement, known as Yom Kippur, the *pesukim* tell us about *inu'im*, understood to mean how we uniquely observe the day with the five *inu'im* of washing, anointing, wearing leather, having relations, and eating. Throughout the verses, there are many instances, especially with regard to the *korbanos*, of the unique status we have and the unique way we relate to Hashem. One example is regarding the prohibition of consuming blood. The *Malbim* views this as a recognition of the role we play in taking responsibility for goodness in the world. How can we justify blood consumption of creatures of the world? What we are allowed to eat and not allowed to eat reflects who we are and how we view ourselves. When a person has a lack of nutritional discipline in allowing himself to partake of any foodstuff regardless of the laws of kashrus, then that impacts his spiritual abilities.

The fact that laws of *tashmish* are codified to preserve our community's morals reflects an overall obligation to maintain a certain level of *kedushah* within our community. Perhaps the most poignant words are "*Va'taki ha'aretz es yoshveha*," which means that the land of Israel reacts to such acts of degradation with a natural expulsion of those who transgress. If we fail to differentiate ourselves and hold ourselves to a higher standard, then a wholly rebuilt Yerushalayim will be out of reach.

The Torah goes so far as to say that this is exactly what the previous residents did to warrant being defeated by the Jewish People. The Almighty is saying, "Do not think that you are immune from these same issues because you are the chosen people, and because you have a special covenant with Me." The only way to be deserving of Eretz Yisrael is to celebrate our Torah lifestyle that sets us apart. It is painfully hard in *galus* to not be influenced by all the secularism that's around us. By reaching out to our fellow Jews to share the beauty of Torah that infuses our life journeys with meaning can successfully help us, on a national level, transform to a broader diaspora community that celebrates how we observe kashrus, Shabbos, *tashmish*, our processes of return (*teshuvah*), and so much more that make us an *Am Kadosh*. With the Almighty's help of assisting in identifying with the values of our *sidrah*, then we will merit the worthiness of being a united people within our eternal holy cities in Israel!

KEDOSHIM

As was discussed last week, part of the agenda of our mitzvos is to create the *kedushah* that exists within the *Am Kadosh*. Connected with that objective is a separate and distinct imperative to create a community infused with *kedushah* apart from mitzvos. In other words, a person can lack *kedushah* while still abiding by all the mitzvos. This concept and category are known as a "*navel b'reshus haTorah.*" The *Ramban* describes how the expectation to be a nation of holy people was emphasized specifically when the people were gathered en masse for *hakhel* because we needed to have as many people included as possible in order be worthy of this mitzvah, which stated in the plural that you "shall be holy." Creating *d'veikus*, as the *Ramban* describes, can't be done by individuals but rather must be done through the power of multitudes. This "clinging" of us to the Almighty, and vice versa, is dependent upon our lives mirroring, in some fashion, the nature of the Almighty as the source of holiness.

The *Netziv* finds an application of this as it related to the transgression of *nosar* (eating from the sacrifices after the time for consumption has elapsed). In other words, one was eating just for the sake of eating without heed for the halachos. Fascinatingly, a different commandment of giving reproach is found in these passages as well, perhaps as a vehicle to accomplish the broad call for holiness. A Jew is required to take responsibility for his fellow and to help amend his errors. The mitzvah of giving *tochachah* is only to be done when it won't be resented.

Wisdom requires a willingness to be shown improvement; conversely, Chazal tell us that it's an **equal** obligation to not give *tochachah* when it can be taken the wrong way, as much as it is to have given *tochachah* in the first place.

The strategy of being each other's teachers is a way for us to jointly avoid the condemnation and the punishment that comes along with the rebelliousness against the Almighty. More so than any other people, the Jewish People are in one ship. It's impossible for half the ship to be sinking and the other half to be floating. Often, we are unintentionally in a bubble and seemingly unaware of how Jews are doing elsewhere. Our *sidrah* describes a truly broad national agenda of holiness and relays how to achieve that through reaching out inspirationally to others. *Parashas Kedoshim* underscores that holiness can't be had by oneself, but rather through *tochachah* and responsible selflessness a *d'veikus* can be ours. May the Almighty help us grow into a people even more worthy of the description *Am Kadosh*!

EMOR

In our *sidrah*, we are warned against desecrating the name of Hashem, and we are also commanded to sanctify Hashem's name. However, when referencing the positive commandment, the verse states, *"V'nikdashti b'soch B'nei Yisrael,"* which means that Hashem states that the sanctification will take place within our community. The very next topic then describes the requirements of the *mo'adim* and the unique rules within the calendar. Yeshayahu HaNavi (see 1:11–14 et al.) relays to us that Hashem detests the holidays when we are in a state of rebellion. How horrifying it is for us to consider how these special days on our calendar could possibly be turned from days of wholesome joy with our families to days in which the Almighty remembers that we are in denial of our own faith nationally. Indeed, we should recall that the holiday calendar is set by *beis din*, which is a halachic body representative of all Klal Yisrael.

The model of *mo'adim* is Shabbos day, and here too our *sidrah* reiterates that all our combined dwellings, *"b'chol moshvoseichem,"* need to be at rest. This turns Shabbos from a personal experience into a broader one, where the Torah charges us to not be callous to our surroundings. The *Seforno* clarifies that desisting from work gives time for Torah matters like studying and learning, which in turn fills the day with *kedushah*. Of course, this is related to the *sidrah*'s reference to *bris olam*, where the community as a whole needs to work together towards fortifying the covenant.

Lastly, during this week's passage of Sukkos, we have a famous midrash that goes into great detail how bringing together the four species is representative of bringing together the different kinds of Jews that exist across the spectrum. Just like you can't have Sukkos without all four species, you can't have a Jewish People without all the types of Jews coming together. Pesach, as well, maintains this air of inclusivity, as we're told by the Rishonim (*Ritva* on Haggadah) that the famous four expressions of redemption correspond to all four types of children who need to be present at our Seder. (Our commentaries also reference this theme when discussing *Ha Lachma Anya* as well). Let's reach out to bring all Jews to a point where our community can truly become a repository for *shalom* so that we can experience "*haShechinah shoreh beineihem*" as implored by Yeshayahu, and thereby be worthy of "*v'nikdashti b'soch B'nei Yisrael*"!

BEHAR

Our *sidrah* this week contains one of the secrets to outreach, which is to reach out early and often, because according to the midrash, trying to lift someone after its too late is five times harder. This is taught by *Rashi* in reference to those who are downtrodden, and the commentary links financial well-being to spiritual well-being. One example of this is Shabbos, and, in our case, it's the restful Shabbos of the agricultural seventh year. Shabbos doesn't belong to the individual but is rather called "*Shabbos laShem.*" It's a Shabbos of *shemittah* that only exists as the intended Shabbos if it's observed by everyone, and not if it's only observed by, let's say, just half the landowners. If, for instance, the land of Israel only has one farmer letting his land lie fallow, then proportionally it accomplishes very little (*Midrash Tanchuma, Vayikra* 1:1). Similarly, education for the seventh day of the week needs to be more prolific, like how the education of *shemittah* has spread throughout all farmers in Israel regardless of observance. Just like the *rasha* excludes himself at the Pesach Seder from the rest of the family by denying involvement in the Exodus experience, so too all Jews are a part of the Shabbos community up until a similar informed rejection takes place. In other words, the analogy is that a person can't exclude himself and be seen as an outcast unless they're aware of our story and collective identity. All children are uniquely bonded based on who their parents are, and all Jews are uniquely bonded based on one of the primary themes of Shabbos, namely our creation as a people in Mitzrayim.

One practical application of this aforementioned discussion on interconnectedness that's found in our *sidrah* is *onaah*, which refers to causing pain to others. It's possible to catch people unaware in business and have a transaction proceed that is not mutually beneficial, thereby harming one of the parties. Similarly, it's possible to verbally hurt an individual, who takes unique exception to an insulting statement or phrase. Based on our common backgrounds, it's a specific transgression to hurt those whose plight one ought to be sympathetic to as if they were our siblings. Similarly, our *sidrah* discusses the different rules of indentured servitude as it pertains to our fellow Jews versus unrelated non-Jews. There are many such examples where kinship is required to be recognized.

Hashem expects us to work toward developing a finished product of Klal Yisrael that reflects these intersectional realities of our unique peoplehood. Shabbos is not just "*lachem*," but also "*laShem*," and to follow through on only one of those would be incompletely dispensing our obligation (*Shemos* 35:2). Just like how we talk to one another and how we treat each other monetarily are governed by our common denominator of Torah and mitzvos, so too our Shabbos experience during the week and even agriculturally as well are representative of the ideas of interdependency that are taught to us by this week's topic of *shemittah.* A starker way of putting it is that if only half the community kept Shabbos, then it can't be said that the community kept Shabbos. May the Almighty help us reach out to one another so that we gain a stronger team effort to keep Shabbos and the other mitzvos more broadly as it pertains to the destiny of our people!

BECHUKOSAI

In relatively plain speech, our *sidrah* spells out that if the Jewish People listen to Hashem's word, then the Almighty will reside within our communities and will turn toward us with Divine providence. More impressively, though, is that the expression of the verse is not just "reside," but also "*v'hishalachti b'sochechem*," and *Rashi* cites Chazal's interpretation that Hashem will accompany us throughout our daily lives. The Rishonim point out that it's up to us whether the Almighty is with us or against us. It's a choice that's presented to us. Essentially, we are to ask ourselves if our communities are compatible with G-dliness. Again, the Torah reiterates the Egypt experience and gives us an ultimatum whether we wish to distinguish ourselves from those around us or whether we want to choose to be like the other nations that have no emancipation experience that warrants the Almighty's special attention.

This existential question—whether we will take responsibility for the Jewish People's relationship with the Almighty—was posed by Yeshayahu quite dramatically, "How did the faithful city get involved with harlotry?" In other words, how did our people get to a place where we were treacherous and disloyal to our Father in Heaven? Yeshayahu singles out murder as one of the main culprits for the decline of Torah that led to a lack of providence. This extreme example involves a callousness where the fate of my fellow fails to matter to the populace. Basic justice involves a community intent to have order, but a city can't have order unless there exists basic levels of affinity and affection one for another. In other words, distrust breeds discontent, which eventually leads to discord and dysfunction.

Our *sidrah* is clear that if we are to have the Almighty's grace and countenance, then we can't be strangers. Uniquely, we believe that the power is ours to decide whether or not we will acknowledge that we are accountable to the Almighty. Our fate is determined based on our collective deservedness. May the Almighty allow us to read our *sidrah* with the broad shoulders needed to be inspired to work toward a complete redemption, based on our collective worthiness for a rebuilt Yerushalayim soon in our days!

SEFER BAMIDBAR

BAMIDBAR

The book of *Bamidbar* begins with an accounting of the nation. *Rashi* comments that this census was taken out of love for the Jewish People. Every person is precious in G-d's eyes. It's incumbent upon us to have a similar valuation of Klal Yisrael. This affinity is occasionally categorized as akin to a spousal partnership. The betrothal was *Matan Torah*, the mountain was the chuppah, and the inaugural *Mishkan* was like the home a couple first enters together (Mishnah, *Kesubos* 4:5). The *Kli Yakar* explains that the *Mishkan* couldn't be inaugurated before a calculation determining a minimum number of Jews and a diversity of camps were present. This was required before the Almighty was *m'asher Shechinaso*. What is *hashraas haShechinah*? It's certainly impossible to know the full extent of the meaning of G-d living among us, however, the *mefarshim* explain that, in order to have a meaningful "marriage" with the Almighty, we need to be together in our worthiness as devoted and loyal subjects of Hashem in service of His will. The *Kli Yakar* continues that the providence of each Jew is equal in weight to entire nations of the world. Only the power of Jews grouped together en masse can lead to the potential we have to be Hashem's bride in this world.

Similarly, Chazal tell us that the Jewish People were able to produce a *Mishkan* of tremendous value to the world. When unified, we can be a great source of strength for humanity, so much so that our sages convey that if the other countries knew what the *Beis Ha'bechirah* provided them, they would use their own defense funds and personnel to guard the Beis Hamikdash. Rav Yehoshua ben Levi, who is the author of this opinion, even goes as far to say that it's more valuable for them than it is to us!

It's hard to understand rationally how providing housing for G-d works, but it's sufficient to say that, for practical purposes, we see how critical it is for Am Yisrael to see the goodness in one another so that we can unite under this unique marital home as established thousands of years ago. May the Almighty provide for us the keen insight to see how we can grow our affection for different strands of Jews and enlighten one another in service of *d'var Hashem*!

NASO

The blessings of the Kohanim appear in our *sidrah* and make reference to Hashem turning towards us as an indication of us meriting *berachah* in our lives. The *Netziv* explains that the concept of Hashem's countenance refers to others seeing within us a tendency to attribute our successes to the Almighty and to Torah, as opposed to the good fortune of our own talents. In other words, when we reach out to others, it's critical that we bring *kavod Shamayim* into our interpersonal dealings. People should see that we are not crediting ourselves, but rather, as Jews, we are products of the Almighty's kindness. We are meant to live so that our neighbors can recognize *hashgachah* through how we act and go about our business. The *Netziv* says that, ideally, once one's acquaintances can perceive this, then, naturally, they will expect you to help them with their own relationship with the Almighty. The consequence of this indirect inspiration is a chain reaction that has the potential to impact all of Am Yisrael. One takeaway is that Jews do not exist in a vacuum, and we uniquely function as a team. The commentaries explain that if we are sincere in our dealings with the Almighty, then it will show on our face, and that's why there's an emphasis within these powerful benedictions to the *panim*. Of course, this is only true if there's sincerity.

The Kohanim conclude their *berachos* with peace, and Rabbeinu Bachya emphasizes that *shalom* is an important ingredient for success as a civilization. Peace is always a joint effort. Certainly, peace starts at home and even with oneself, but overall *shalom* is a more global matter. The commentary continues that Shlomo HaMelech only excelled in his G-d-given wisdom because of the tranquility that surrounded him and because he was able to facilitate a calm throughout the citizenry. Besides *panim* and *shalom*, there is the term "*ya'er*," which means to enlighten. It is no coincidence that Aharon was responsible for the illumination of the *Menorah* and was gifted that responsibility because of the healing that he brought between people at odds with one another. (One example of the connection between light and peace can be found from prioritizing the mitzvah of Shabbos candles.) Lastly, the service of *Birkas Kohanim* is customarily only held daily in the land of Israel, because Klal Yisrael only warrants these special utterances when there is tranquility and opportunity to come together as a focused community. The land of Israel is endowed with these qualities, as are these special days on our calendar, for we are "home," both in a geographic and calendric sense.

Immediately following *Birkas Kohanim* is a description of the physical lifting that was expected of the Kohanim subgroups for the *Mishkan*. The amount they had to carry varied and was "*k'fi avodasam*," which, perhaps, homiletically could mean that all bring their different strengths to the equation of service to Hashem. Let's read our *sidrah* carefully so that we learn the Torah's concept of Aharon-like *tzidkus* so that what we strive for includes a growth-oriented approach that invites others to come along with us. May the Almighty keep us connected so that we have a Solomonic peace that allows all the disparate Jewish groups to come in unison under Torah to bring *chochmah* into the world.

BEHAALOSECHA

Our *sidrah* discusses the mitzvah of the *Korban Pesach*, which is the mitzvah that requires all Jews to break off into groups in order to come together to partake in eating from the Paschal lamb, which is in commemoration of the great miracles wrought on our behalf in Mitzrayim. Perhaps, this is the mitzvah that stresses the notion of "no Jew left behind," since everyone has to be with his own *chaburah* without exception. Our *sidrah* further delineates that if one was exceptionally precluded from partaking because he was *tamei*, then Hashem tasked Moshe explicitly with an additional ordinance to allow for a make-up date on the following month. The words that underscore the critical nature of this inclusion are, "*kol kahal adas Yisrael*," which means every member of the tribe. It was critical for all the Jews to be a part of the message that the Almighty's Omnipotence was most apparent during the Exodus, thus proving His dominion to the world. Even on this rain date, matzoh and maror are required along with the additional rule of multiple people being in attendance (see *Minchas Chinuch* 380).

The *Ohr Hachaim* explains that the equality of the convert is reiterated with this mitzvah of Pesach Sheini because of his lack of history in Egypt. The commentator further clarifies that one might have thought that there are certain mitzvos less relevant to the *ger*, and so the Torah wants to make very clear the radical retroactive reality that a convert post-facto was equally present in Egypt ("*geulas olam gam l'nefesh ha'ger*"). These mitzvos of our *sidrah* are singled out as the means through which we come to embrace the inclusivity of Jewry, and that all those new to the community are brought to the innermost circles of even the bondage commemorations as per the Pesach-offering commandments. "*Chukah achas*" is written here to emphasize that we are all alike under G-d's law, regardless of our personal backgrounds (*Sifri, Bamidbar* 71).

One of the inhibitions blocking us from doing a better job at bringing our Jewish communities together with Torah is that we mistakenly think that the Torah views different demographics differently. The truth, as illustrated by this week's *sidrah*, is that irrespective of our religious backgrounds, who our parents are, what educational institutions we attended, or what our social connections are like, that doesn't put us into different categories. Furthermore, the lesson of Pesach Sheini is that some can be rendered *tamei* or dealt a bad hand precluding their involvement for a temporary duration of time, but it logically follows that our communities and our leaders will be held accountable if avenues aren't made available for accessing our birthright. May the Almighty endow our Torah communities with vision and with solutions for attracting as many Jews as possible to the Torah routines that define Klal Yisrael!

SHELACH

In our *sidrah*, we read of the extraordinary rise and fall of the *meraglim*. These men, leaders and representatives of each tribe, were selected to scout out the Promised Land. This was the yearning for hundreds of years of heartbroken, enslaved, men, women, and children. The *meraglim* returned with a report that dashed the hopes of the *dor ha'midbar.* These men were not just castigated and rightfully punished because of their own personal actions but all the more so because of the impact they had on the community. They failed to appreciate the positive impact they could have had in influencing the congregation of Israel, and that gravely missed opportunity is what led to their demise. The inability to effect progress for Klal Yisrael whenever feasible can result in devastating culpability.

The result of their actions and the words of the conversation that led to Moshe achieving another salvation for Am Yisrael provides great insight into the horrible tensions that erupted as a result of the spies' fatal error. The *Ohr Hachaim* points out that we see through Moshe's successful defense and advocacy on our behalf that the concern was not the disparaging remarks about Israel but rather the desecration of G-d's name. How the Jewish People act and the events that befall us cause a ripple effect around the world. Moshe utilizes the imagery of "*k'ish echad*"; the Almighty can exact revenge against our treachery like a vengeance taken all at once against Am Yisrael, as if we were one man—not to underscore the ease by which the Almighty can act, but rather the unity with which we exist in the world. We choose to either take or not take responsibility for each other wherever we might be and at our own peril. Because of our unique existence and mission as a people, our oneness is our precondition for bringing the highest levels of *kiddush Hashem*, or *chas v'shalom*, *chillul Hashem*. It's worth adding that, while the Almighty extracted us from the cauldron of a slavery that could have wiped us out, it came with a string attached: We were only saved on condition—for the purposes of being a tool to spread the wisdom of Torah around the globe. It is this concept portrayed by Moshe that leads to the greatest pardon in our history (14:15). We invoke these words of "*salachti ki'devarecha*" on the Day of Atonement for a similar forgiveness (see *Ramban* 14:17). Often times, we invoke these same phrases (14:18–19) for our own spiritual cleanliness and *teshuvah* goals during Yom Kippur. However, the *meraglim* led a national *chillul Hashem*, not just through a personal mistake of focusing negatively on the land, but by focusing on the people as a whole. They were guilty of comparing Am Yisrael to lowly and weak *chagavim*, easily crushable insects (*Sifsei Chachamim* 13:33).

In conclusion, to borrow from American lore, "We must all hang together, or, most assuredly, we shall all hang separately." In other words, our ability to come together and see the best in each other will determine our success as the Am Hashem. The midrash reinforces this with its interpretation of our verse, "*Torah achas u'mishpat echad yihiyeh lachem*," which is understood to mean that all Jewish People are equal and, in particular, are equal when it comes to Torah. In our case, the spies failed to realize Chazal's philosophy of "*d'gufa basar reisha azil*," which means the body follows the head, and when a majority of Klal Yisrael errs, it is the leadership and the nation that are required together to orchestrate a macro-level repentance.

Lastly, we see that Kalev and Yeshoshua were spared punishment and were allowed to enter Israel with the next generation. The Gemara tells us the secret of Kalev, who didn't benefit from being Moshe's disciple like Yehoshua, was that he went to Chevron to derive inspiration from the Avos and Imahos. Throughout our *sidrah*, we have a theme of Jewish interconnectedness that fills our *pesukim*. May the Almighty allow us to crystallize for ourselves the fundamental idea that we exist as a unified force of many different demographics, past, present, and future, to unite in Torah to build each other up equally for progress in our eternal mission. With that, we will experience, "*v'nislach **l'chol adas Yisrael***," and surely with Hashem's pardon once again, we will be able to achieve a *geulah sheleimah*!

KORACH

The insurrection led by Korach provides a great lesson for reaching out more to each other so that we better appreciate our collective providence. Korach said, "*kulam kedoshim*," that all Jews are holy, which was meant not as much as praise but rather as a challenge to Moshe's leadership. The verse tells us that the rebels didn't like Moshe and Aharon lording over them, but only Moshe "fell on his face" in response to these threats. Why did Aharon not respond in kind, and why did Moshe fall on his face instead of answering them? The answer is that Korach's words had some truth, thereby making his defiance more difficult to be dealt with by the leadership (*Rashi* 16:3). Therefore, Moshe fell on his face in prayer to see from Hashem what the most effective response could be, and Aharon saw the rightness of Korach's stance, albeit of a twisted call for equality, as *Rashi* explains that, after all, the Almighty revealed Himself to all the people at Har Sinai.

Rashi comments that indeed all had prophetic powers and capabilities, as evidenced by the revelation at Har Sinai. So, Moshe could not accordingly choose and place one Jew over another. It would have to be up to Hashem, and it would entirely be determined by Hashem's demonstration. We learn from Moshe's actions that, even in the most extreme cases, a Jew is never allowed to excise another Jew or group of Jews without the Almighty's Torah diktat. If ever there was a time to take action to excommunicate a group of rabble rousers, it would have been Moshe's put-down of this revolution. Alas, Moshe teaches us, in his deference to Hashem, that only Hashem can determine the status of individuals within the *Am Kadosh*. This concept is echoed by Shmuel HaNavi when he states explicitly, "*Hashem meimis u'mechayeh morid she'ol va'yaal*," which the Gemara interprets to mean that Hashem decides both in this world and in the next world (see *Sanhedrin* 108a). We shouldn't take it upon ourselves to determine someone's spiritual and physical existence. The Sages describe further that Moshe was not just hesitant to act but tried as much as he could to convince them to backtrack. There was no kneejerk, instinctual reaction to banish them as would have been deserving, since Moshe understood the secret to Jewish power being a fully intact tribe. If they stayed together and had as many contributors as possible, then they would be able to achieve greatness. Only as a last resort, when this troublesome poison threatened to spread, did Moshe ask Hashem for an intervention to "amputate" and excise as needed. This provided a timeless lesson that reverberates today, as relayed to us by Chazal (*Vayikra Rabbah* 4:6):

> *Chizkiyahu taught (Yirmiyahu 50:17): "Israel are scattered sheep"; why are Israel likened to a sheep? Just as a sheep, when hurt on its head or on another part of its body, all of its body parts feel it, so it is with Israel, when one of them sins, everyone feels it: "When one man sins [will You be wrathful with the whole community] (Bamidbar 16:22)." Rabbi Shimon bar Yochai taught a parable: Men were on a ship. One of them took a drill and started drilling underneath him. The others said to him: What are you sitting and doing?! He replied: What do you care? Is this not underneath my area that I am drilling?! They said to him: But the water will rise and flood us all on this ship. This is as Iyov said (Iyov 19:4): "If indeed I have erred, my error remains with me." But his friends said to him (Iyov 34:37): "He adds transgression to his sin; he extends it among us." [The men on the ship said]: You extend your sins among us.*

The *Ramban* dramatically describes the full extent of the implications when indicating that Hashem was truly determined to bring down the entire nation of Israel. He explains that just like Hashem used a plague to kill the firstborn in Egypt while leaving alive the individual next to him, the intention here was to hold the entire Jewish People responsible for the insurgency that was rapidly becoming popular; the community was, therefore, under advisement to separate themselves to avoid the danger, because the Almighty had no plans to spare them. May the Almighty give us the deftness to appreciate the *kedushah* of our people for the good and not for the bad. And May the Almighty help us internalize our linked fates as members of a holy people spared due to the exploits of Moshe Rabbeinu who saw our great promising future.

CHUKAS

Our *sidrah's* discussion of Moshe creating a copper snake is a study in Moshe utilizing a psychological trigger to serve as a catalyst that would lead to introspection and reflection. This extreme tactic might have been considered idolatrous had it not been ordered by the Ribbono Shel Olam. The consideration for us is what can we do to attune the focus of our communities in the absence of these measures. Some verses later, we're told that emissaries were sent by Israel to seek peace from Sichon to avoid conflict. First, while a health or military crisis exists, there can't be growth by citizenry. Second, the commentaries explain that since it didn't say Moshe sent the emissaries himself, that teaches us that Moshe and the people were on the same page. The people are their leadership and vice versa (*Midrash Tanchuma* 23). For those who seek to be leaders and not followers for the sake of Torah success, it behooves us to note *Rashi's* quote of the midrash, "*Nasi ha'dor k'chol ha'dor*," which means that the leader is considered analogous to the entire generation. Similarly, when Amalek attacked us, Moshe raised his hands to the Heavens, precipitating gains on the battlefield. Our sages explain that it's not his hands that led us to victory but rather the visual effect of having guided the Jewish soldiers' thoughts toward the direction of the Heavens, and thus closer to the Almighty, that made them worthy of vanquishing the enemy. (See *Mechilta* in *Beshalach* for further explanation of intersectionalism of leadership and Am Yisrael.)

Conversely, when Moshe struck the rock instead of speaking to it to bring forth water, Moshe's lack of leadership had a negative impact on the faith of the people. *Rashi* explains that the masses would have concluded that a rock that cannot hear has listened to the will of the Almighty, so then they too should give focus to listening to the will of their Creator. The *Baal Haturim* (1269–1343) comments that it wasn't that Moshe's actions lessened their *emunah*, rather, it was the lost opportunity of raising *kavod Shamayim* within the ranks of Am Yisrael. The ensuing admonishment and punishment were warranted for Moshe and Aharon, who were responsible for their generation's faith.

One has to ask himself whether the Torah community is doing all it can to prevent an erosion, and what opportunities are being missed to bolster Torah in our own generation. From the days of Moshe until the times of Rabban Gamliel in the Talmud, whenever they would study Torah, they would stand to honor the experience that they were partaking in, but today we do not have that stamina. Standing out of respect signifies and symbolizes to all those around us of our desire to rise to be *mekadesh sheim Shamayim.* May the Almighty grant our communities a spirit of ingenuity to best determine how to activate this inspiration that the Jewish People desperately need to turn our hearts closer to Hashem!

BALAK

Our *sidrah* gives us a stern warning about not losing our sense of self. If we assimilate, then we risk who we are as a people. While we need to be friendly within the world of nations, we always need to set up certain boundaries that prevent us from being susceptible to foreign ideologies and influences. This week, we read about the assimilation that took place with Moav, where Jews and gentiles became too intimately acquainted. The commentaries explain that, if we're in Israel, on our own land, or by ourselves in the desert, being influenced by other value systems is not a concern relative to when we live among other peoples. We are uniquely impressionable, and the Moabite women were successful in drawing the men towards licentious idolatry. The midrash explains that the *pasuk* gives us what appears to be unimportant information regarding in which city this atrocity took place, however, Shittim is actually related to the word "*shtus*," which means that it was a city of frivolity (*Bamidbar Rabbah* 20:22, based on *Mishlei* 6:32). What appears to be innocuous can actually be very harmful, as it can cause a Torah Jew to be less connected to his Torah observances.

Rabbeinu Yonah (1200–1263) writes that Pinchas, who acted with zealotry to dramatically bring an end to the moral rebelliousness, is someone who should be emulated. Just like Pinchas sought to act to preserve the spiritual integrity of Am Yisrael, so too "all G-d fearing people are obligated" to assist our community's leaders, when appropriate, to carry out interventions as necessary to preserve Klal Yisrael. In other words, all Jews need to take responsibility for each other and not just leave it to others to take care of national matters of importance. We learn about this mutual bond in part from the previous failed attempt of Bilaam to curse Klal Yisrael, where the Almighty causes him to declare the goodness of Jewish tents and dwellings, which references our houses of study and worship, respectively. The secret to our success is congregation under the roofs of Torah, as detailed by our adversary in the *sidrah*. Without places to congregate in prayer and education for Torah concepts, there can't be an internalization and a concretizing of our *hashkafos*. Ultimately, Bilaam was successful in tragically seeing the demise of twenty-four thousand Jews during the plague following the rebellion. Bilaam was known to be involved in deviant, amoral relations and wished to have the Jews stoop to his level. As we see at the end of the *sidrah*, he succeeded in enticing Jews, drawing them away from these Jewish Torah infrastructures.

Our nemeses, Bilaam and Balak, knew they had to break up our connection to the Almighty and worked hard towards severing that relationship. Our enemies tried militarily overwhelming us or turning towards their black magical forces, but Balak specifically wanted a prophet and was trying to time it right using his wisdom to ascertain our spiritual missteps. They knew that they were powerless against us unless they could activate our Achilles' heel, causing us to transgress and stray from the ways of the Torah. It's important for us to read about these ploys every year so that we focus on the strength that we need to draw from one another as we too combat the influences of the diaspora that seek to undermine our sense of a strong identity in ways that pull us from Torah observance. Only a united Jewish People, congregating in our shuls and schools, will allow us to be effective in maintaining a familiarity with our timeless, exceptional character.

PINCHAS

Rav Noach Weinberg used to say that if one evil person had the ability to inspire a holocaust of our people, then certainly the Almighty equally endowed man with the comparable potential to save our people. If Pinchas was endowed with such abilities to halt our destruction in his generation, then a single Jew today can similarly accomplish such a feat (see *Sanhedrin* 38 and *Pirkei D'Rebbi Eliezer* 47). Our sages teach us that Pinchas was not dissuaded from action despite the fact that he was not among the leaders of the Jewish People. He didn't let his youth or being three generations removed from the top get in the way of what needed to be done. The purity and sincerity that he exhibited have much to do with why our oral tradition equates Pinchas with Eliyahu HaNavi. At great risk, Pinchas took vengeance against a tribal leader, Zimri ben Salu of Shevet Shimon. He was concerned about Hashem's honor and not his own personal, familial interests. Chazal tell us that his mother was a convert, and, on his father's side, they also didn't have to go through slavery, since he was from Shevet Levi. He knew that if he acted with conviction, Am Yisrael would respect his act and return to their senses as G-d-fearing servants of the Almighty (*Netziv* 25:13).

The *Akeidas Yitzchak* (1420–1494) explains that Pinchas was the consummate hero because he saw that his life would not be worth living had he not acted to prevent a world from materializing that would have forever altered morality for himself and his people. Many miracles were wrought on Pinchas' behalf. Obviously, he never acted for the sake of such a reward, but these wonders mark for us the exploits that should be emulated. Maybe our actions won't be as dramatic, and hopefully not as violent, but rather similar in terms of magnitude and piety. The *Ramban* explains that because Pinchas was in awe of the Almighty, instead of the great royalty status of Zimri and Cozbi, he merited an eternal *kehunah* through his progeny. He disregarded those who might say his father and Zimri should be in the same classification. He saw that Klal Yisrael's enemies were weaponizing intermarriage to subvert a Jewish future, so he knew he had to take action (*Bamidbar Rabbah* 20).

Similarly, in our *sidrah*, the daughters of Tzelophchad respectfully challenged authority to save an entire demographic of Jews from not possessing land in Israel. They saw with clarity and courage that the Jewish People had to be whole and intact, and those left on the outside without equal rights would make our people deficient, thereby undermining our national mission. They had no connection to leadership, but their virtuous innovation led them to be referred to by the Gemara as *chachmanios*, *darshanios*, and *tzidkanios*, which means masters of wisdom, interpretation, and righteousness, respectively. Lastly, Moshe's act of selflessness in whole-heartedly appointing Yehoshua as a successor without insistence on his own family's patrilineal descent marks a third example this week of putting Klal Yisrael as a priority above smaller, individual concerns. May the Almighty give us the astuteness and sensitivity to see our *sidrah* as a means to conceive the plans to best serve our generation's challenges in the assimilation of our *galus* so that we might yet taste the fruits of redemption in Eretz Yisrael.

MATOS

In this week's *sidrah*, we learn about the laws of vows and obligating oneself through personal oaths. *Rashi*'s comments on the technicality of a husband's erroneous annulment the day after his wife's vow, leading to him replacing her in culpability should the vow be violated. *Rashi*'s words are, "*Ha'goreim takalah l'chaveiro hu nichnas tachtav*," which means that causing mistakes to another person results in standing in for your fellow's liability. The midrash derives from this discussion that the opposite must likewise be true, that one who causes goodness to his neighbor realizes such reward as well. How can one replace his fellow in the negative just by giving bad advice, or in the positive through enabling others via good advice?

The *Ramban* explains that the concept of taking a punishment for another's transgression only applies when there's an opportunity to do something about it and counter the *cheit*. Similarly, we have to ask ourselves if there's anything we can do to stem the tide of assimilation where we live. When Moshe needs to select men for the campaign against Midian to save Klal Yisrael, the *Ramban* says that he specifically selects those who were *tzaddikim*. Maybe, one would have thought he should leave the righteous behind to protect them from injury or worse. Maybe let them stick to their studies to preserve them for internal, communal responsibilities? Maybe send others for their brawn and military muscle? Moshe's strategy showcases that our people's existence is determined by ambassadors of Torah standing up for Klal Yisrael. The recipe for similar progress is timeless just as our collective constitution and our covenant with the Almighty is a constant.

Later in our *sidrah*, Moshe questions the moral fiber of Gad and Reuven when they request permission to settle the Transjordan, thereby presumably leaving the conquest expedition of Eretz Yisrael to others to undertake. The *Ohr Hachaim* explains that the issue was not just a seeming callousness, but rather, in order for Am Yisrael to thrive, there needs to be a complete participation from all the *Shevatim* and all the segments of the citizenry. The result of Moshe's admonition is an express commitment by Gad and Reuven to stay until every Jew is taken care of and settled in the mainland. In other words, when a shul or community exists in solidarity with all the different segments of Klal Yisrael, then it will be *zocheh* to be redeemed in Eretz Yisrael. May the Almighty give us the strength to empower each of our leaders to preserve and to assist the Jewish People in accessing the *berachos* promised via earnest Torah performance.

MAS'EI

In our *sidrah*, the stops in the journey across the *midbar* are delineated, including the moment when the valiant Aharon Hakohen passes away. With his death, the Clouds of Glory that had loyally protected Klal Yisrael disappeared. The Gemara tells us that the king of Arad heard about our leader's passing immediately, despite the encampment being far away. Chazal explain that he was told the news by his scouts, who informed him that this special cloud shielding Am Yisrael from its enemies had been lifted. Similarly, the Torah tells us that all the Jewish People saw that Aharon had been gathered up by his Creator, which is impossible since he expired on the mountain, and they couldn't have all borne witness to this event. The Talmud tells us that the nation saw this protective cover depart from them. Moreover, the king of Arad saw our defenses were down and thought to himself that the G-d of the Jews was indicating our vulnerability so that he could initiate an attack. Because Aharon made peace between neighbors, it was in his merit that we had peace and weren't susceptible to our enemies. After Aharon's death, though, we would need to earn Hashem's providence more directly.

The Almighty tells us later in our *sidrah* to clean house of all the idolatry in the land of Israel. Our safety and security would depend on how thorough we would be. Our commentaries understand that peace in Eretz Yisrael is dependent upon our ability to drive deviant philosophies away from our communities. This massive undertaking can only be accomplished with a robust national commitment, as there is no longer a Moshe or Aharon to save us from the Almighty's judgments.

Lastly, the legacy of Aharon ultimately still impacted our worthiness of settling in tranquility. The descendants of Aharon were to administer the cities of refuge. This week's reading about the *arei miklat* leads us to the conclusion that setting up residences for the unwanted, the accidental killers of society, would be a prerequisite for having our own country. Naturally, the lovers of peace, Aharon's progeny would take in these refugees to Hashem's *arei miklat* because they uniquely understood the value of each Jew, and that character improvements could be made. Our *sidrah* teaches that the ways of Aharon to pursue peace is the manner through which we gain Divine favor and high levels of *hashgachah*. By ridding ourselves of "false gods" and coming together under the canopy of Torah, we'll be able to merit living in our land with Mashiach. The Torah's ways are called *darchei noam*, and as we recite *kol nesivoseha shalom*, meaning whenever we involve ourselves with living our eternal wisdom, then our ability to join as one becomes that much stronger. Then, as the Almighty has promised us, we will be able to live out our days in the rebuilt Eretz Yisrael that had been gifted to our ancestors thousands of years ago.

SEFER DEVARIM

DEVARIM

The *Ramban* explains to us that *Sefer Devarim* communicates what Moshe needed to tell us in order to peacefully live in the land. It doesn't reiterate all of the rules for Kohanim, as much as it reinforces the reassurances and the warnings regarding deviant philosophies such as idolatry. Prior to teaching these mitzvos and some of the mitzvos yet to be taught, Moshe's tactic is to remind the people how much love and kindness the Almighty has bestowed upon them with extraordinary levels of compassion. The *Ramban* continues that they shouldn't get dismayed, and Hashem's tolerance will allow them the opportunity to mend any mistakes made. Klal Yisrael shouldn't live in fear that they will be cast back into the wilderness if they show insincerity in their commitment to Torah. Therefore, *Devarim* is indeed a roadmap and a guide for how to conduct ourselves within our relationship with Hakadosh Boruch Hu. It's also a template for today and the *teshuvah* movement.

An additional idea that can help us further Moshe's mission of encouraging Klal Yisrael to stay confident and to reinforce this week's message in our *sidrah* of Moshe striving to keep us intact even after his demise, is the concept of "*kol Yisrael yeish lahem chelek l'Olam Haba*," which means all of Am Yisrael is worthy of a portion in the World to Come. We might be quick to write off certain individuals or groups who we think are intentionally or unintentionally subverting our loyalty to Torah, but if Hashem doesn't write them off, then certainly we can't afford to forego their material and immaterial contributions that further our people's redemption. This concept is immortalized in the Mishnah in *Sanhedrin*, where we learn the words of Yeshayahu, "*V'ameich kulam tzaddikim*," which means that all of your people are righteous. The Chafetz Chaim explains that what this really means is that, deep down, each Jew really wants to do what's right in the eyes of the Torah were it not for various impediments (see commentary of the *Rambam*, *Sanhedrin* 10:1).

We have to be thankful to the Almighty that *middas ha'rachamim* rules over *middas ha'din*. The Gemara explains that this is the way Jews are supposed to treat others as well. Just like the Almighty doesn't remove Jews from the fold, then certainly we're expected to conduct ourselves accordingly to try and make every excuse possible to broaden the proverbial tent instead of narrowing it, *chas v'shalom*. On the contrary, we must live our lives as Moshe did, trying to make Am Yisrael as worthy as possible. The *Rambam* codifies this into law when he charges the Torah community to energetically bring Jews, who have been born into Jewish illiteracy due to lack of education, closer to their spiritual home of the Torah (*Hilchos Mamrim* 3:3). Those who are distant from Torah almost always fall into the category of *tinok she'nishbah*, whom we are expected to embrace within our collective institutions. May the Almighty give us the appreciation necessary to create an informed and inspired Jewish populace who are committed as one to the *hashkafas haTorah*!

VA'ESCHANAN

In our *sidrah* this week, there are many portals through which we can see the purpose of mitzvos. The *Ran* (1320–1376) and others explain that the words cited at the beginning of the fourth *perek* of "*V'atah Yisrael Shema*" (and now Israel should listen to the laws), imply that love is the basis for the gift of the system of mitzvos (*Sifri*, *Devarim* 30). In other words, it was correctly predicted that many of us would be repeatedly misinformed or look inaccurately at the commandments as burdens. Instead, however, we ought to see the *taryag mitzvos* for what they are, which is evidence of the uniquely loving relationship the Almighty has with all of us. The mitzvos are not so that a king gets served by his subjects, but rather our service is really dictated for our own enjoyment and benefit.

Paradoxically, even though it's for our benefit, mitzvos are incumbent upon us and are obligatory in order to showcase the uplifting wisdom of the Torah (*Yalkut Shimoni*, *Shmuel II* 161). There is a national obligation to display the knowledge and understanding that are meant to be the mark of our people. To be successful in this national endeavor, we need to see for ourselves and share with others the great other-worldly joy of Torah living. Part of fulfilling the *Shema* prayer is doing our part in *Shema Yisrael*, which means to make sure that the Jewish People listen to the call of the oneness of the Ribbono Shel Olam. This doesn't mean to save such responsibilities for rabbis and teachers, but rather for all those required to say the *Shema*, namely everybody. The *Ramban* understands that the *Shema* references tefillin and mezuzah so that our heart (parallel to the arm), head, and homes are inspired with the reality of the Almighty. It doesn't only say "houses," but also "gates," in the last verse of the *Shema*. This refers to the requirement of our towns to ring true to the tune of *Toras emes*. Then, the very next *pasuk* tells us that beyond our deserving nature, should we ensure this congregational wide commitment, there will be enough merit to be in the land of Israel. The *Ralbag* interprets the words "*Shema Yisrael*" as a requirement that if one engages in Torah study, then part of that study needs to have an anticipation of teaching others as well. Just learning about mitzvos is a failed attempt at learning Torah, as implied in *Shema* ***Yisrael***, as it needs to be acted upon and shared (*Abarbanel* 4:1).

The end of the *sidrah* concludes with our obligation to maintain the covenant. Moshe explains that we obviously know, based on history, that the Almighty will take care of all that was promised. The question seemingly remains whether we will take care of all that *we* promised. The mitzvah of saying *Shema* twice a day is not just a required recitation but an internalization that the secret to Jewish survival is to act on our Torah values and to bring them center stage. May the Almighty give us the keen insight necessary to include all our brothers and sisters in establishing a global awareness of the wisdom latent within Torah living.

EIKEV

In our *sidrah*, we learn that man cannot assess the importance of specific actions. Indeed, we are told at the very beginning by *Rashi* that the mitzvos that are commonly trampled by society are the exact ones that will lead to us being the recipients of the promised *chessed* from Hakadosh Baruch Hu. The Mishnah in *Avos* advises us to be just as careful with mitzvos that appear to be more trivial. It's hard to tell if the person raised to keep Shabbos gets more reward based on the number of Shabbosim kept, or if a person who keeps fewer Shabbosim gets more credit for starting to observe Shabbos later in life (see *Nedarim* 39b). One could fill in the blank with many different examples. So explains David HaMelech in *Tehillim* (49:6), where according to the *Daas Zekeinim*, David's concern at the end of his days was about the smaller expectations the Almighty had laid for man, because the bigger ones were known to have been faithfully fulfilled by David HaMelech when looking back on his life. The *Daas Zekeinim* continues that man is ignorant as to how the Almighty will reward our good deeds. The two exceptions to this are honoring parents and shooing away the mother bird before taking her eggs, where we are told about receiving long life. One, *kibbud av v'eim*, was on the *luchos*, and the other, *shiluach ha'ken*, seems relatively trite when compared to venerating those who gave us life. The reason these two very different mitzvos were highlighted was to teach us not to judge required Torah activities ourselves and presumptively ascribe our own value.

Relatedly, we are not in a position to determine the spiritual value of observant lives versus less observant lives because such assessments are done by Hashem. Legendarily, a story is told about a boy who came to join the davening, but only recited the *aleph-beis* because that was all he knew. The townspeople moved to stop this affront to the minyan until the rabbi let it be known that this prayer was of the most value. Allegorically, the same could be said for the actions of our fellow brothers and sisters.

Similarly, the *Kli Yakar* writes the reason why the eighth *perek* begins in the singular and then immediately switches to the plural ("*kol ha'mitzvah…tishmerun…ticheyun*") is that every person who follows through on their mitzvah responsibility has the ability to add vitality to the world around them. One might not have thought that society rises and falls according to his own behaviors, but our *sidrah* teaches us that the world is tangibly better off because one individual made a difference. Perhaps the reason our *sidrah* reviews the breaking of the tablets is to demonstrate that Moshe understood the power we possessed as three million individuals capable of helping the world. Moshe's successful intervention is predicated upon the argument that we could yet fulfill our mission as a people (Rav Hirsch, *Shemos* 34:9).

The *Ramban* reiterates in this week's commentary that the ultimate question of "what does the Almighty want from us" comes down to whether we assimilate and become like the rest of the nations of the world, or whether we recognize that we've been chosen instead of Yishmael and Eisav and other nations. In other words, the Almighty doesn't need empty, superficial performances but rather needs us to see the goodness that can enhance our lives through Torah. The *Ramban* continues with the theological point from Iyov that there's nothing Hashem can receive from humanity that has any value; rather, it is only our society that benefits. This is the message of our *sidrah* that needs to be shared. We do not know which person's particular acts of devotion to our timeless Torah will have the biggest impact, but we do know that all Torah acts will result in uplifting all those around us.

RE'EH

In our *sidrah* this week, we begin with a choice and the ultimate expression of man's power to have free will in order to decide his own direction in life. While people make up their own minds individually, the ultimatum is presented in the plural. This is yet another example that we exist as part of a collective and as part of a body greater than ourselves. Leaders are held responsible for a generation's direction, but each person is accountable for the choices he makes and the outcomes that follow. As the *Rambam* states, we all have the capacity to achieve our potential and, thereby, to be on par with Moshe Rabbeinu (*Hilchos Teshuvah* 5:2). The highest level a human being has the ability to reach is the level of *nevuah*. The ultimate goal of the *neviim*, as seen throughout Tanach, was to eradicate foreign ideas that were antithetical to Torah. Indeed, the *Netziv* writes that our *sidrah* is clear that idolatry needs to be subdued before Torah can be established. No doubt, this is not just for the land of Israel but universally; idolatry and Torah are like oil and water that cannot mix (*Shir Hashirim Rabbah* 1:3).

Too often, people try to determine for themselves what a good religious life might look like, without realizing that they are creating daily routines that are really about convenience and a quasi-worship of self. The *Seforno* explains the word "*re'eh*" as seeing that the Almighty has provided divergent pathways as options for our lives. Most of the world tries to take all that life has to offer to create a journey that offers the least resistance, but a Jew needs to celebrate his identity by recognizing there are some clear right and wrongs. We do not believe that one can do whatever he likes as long as he causes no harm to others because we are all one big family; and sometimes decisions need to be made in every life that will unknowingly impact others. Hashem promises us that our stiff-necked steadfastness to believe in who we are will give us a respect among the nations that will ensure our eternal existence in the world.

Similar to the *Netziv*'s idea of eradicating the negative to allow the positive to flourish, the Chafetz Chaim explains that peace is a prerequisite for a thriving society and that, to achieve health, one often needs to dispose of the poisons in his diet. It's impossible for the Jewish community to deny and close their eyes to how broad a constituency we have, yet working towards educating authentic Judaism is critical to undoing the many fallacies that have unfortunately become a part of who we are via secularism. Obviously, it's ineffectively, sinfully violent to go about unilaterally destroying temples of idolatry, however, it's clearly incumbent upon us to ascertain what would be most effective in reversing trends that promote harmful concepts for civilization. As described this week, a foundation must be firm in all our communities, and foundations can't be laid unless the ground is ripe for building. May the Almighty give us the sense that allows us to appreciate that Am Yisrael is relying on each other to establish stability for the entire base of what we are trying to construct, and that interpersonal amity as well as intellectual harmony are required to rebuild our everlasting dreams of *geulah*.

SHOFTIM

The laws of judges are not just about legal justice and order ascribed to a punitive system to allow for society to function but rather, a Torah society has respectable officers of integrity that are loved for their ability to maintain ethics within a Jewish civic setting. Just like there are regional and district tiers for judicial systems within halachah, so too there are such infrastructure demands for schooling as conveyed by the *Rambam* (*Hilchos Sanhedrin* 1:1, *Hilchos Talmud Torah* 2:1). All municipalities need educational institutions, and the obligatory language used for both is very similar. This seems like a very daunting and demanding task to ensure proper *chinuch* for all Jewish students, yet the midrash explains this week that no matter how daunting, we need not be afraid.

Talmud Torah is often compared to an intellectual war, *milchamta shel Torah* (see *Rashi*, *Sotah* 7b). We must have courage in the course of this *milchemes Hashem* as we strive with determination *l'sheim Shamayim.* Indeed, the original battle waged by Avraham on behalf of Hashem against the four kings was simply himself and Eliezer versus considerably more formidable forces. The *Chizkuni* (1250–1310) explains that, for war efforts, there is always a role for every soldier, no matter the conflict. The same can be said and should be said for the battle against ignorance and assimilation. And, when the stakes are as high as they are today, there are no excuses. Indeed, the physical life of any member of Klal Yisrael is meant to be treated with the highest levels of seriousness, and the same is absolutely true for one's spiritual life. Interestingly, the midrash cites our *sidrah* for the reunification of Am Yisrael. When Yaakov Avinu is faced with the brothers' startling assertions Yosef is alive, and he ponders if, alas, Yosef is indeed still alive, whether physically or spiritually, he is only convinced when he sees the *agalos* that Yosef sent, which were reminiscent of the *sugya* of *egla arufa*. Only then he knew that this was really his long-lost son, who had not been swallowed, nor spiritually overwhelmed, by the diaspora that he had been sold to, and that his Torah helped preserve him in exile.

Lastly, the *Sefer Hachinuch* comments on this week's *sidrah* that the commandment to preserve nature, and specifically to not destroy fruit trees, is connected to increasing Torah. Part of the mitzvah is not just to guard against wanton destruction but to emulate the people of piety who love peace. The *Sefer Hachinuch* writes, "*Semeichim b'tuv ha'briyos u'mekarvin osan la'Torah v'lo yoveidu afilu gargar shel chardal ba'olam.*" These models of excellence are those who gladden others and bring them close to Torah and would never even lay waste to one mustard seed in the world. For these individuals recognize that they are given *kochos* (abilities) to prevent loss of Creation. They recognize that their uniqueness stems from an overall outlook of preventing waste and staying away from the philosophy that misery loves company. In other words, there's an overall Torah approach to care for the world and most importantly to care for others. While it's not easily intuitive that this mitzvah is connected to drawing those closer to Torah, the *Sefer Hachinuch* comes to teach us that it's all the same mentality of getting the most out of this G-d-gifted world. If you care about people, then, certainly, you'll act responsibly with the environment, and, all the more so, with the inhabitants and brothers and sisters surrounding us who are thirsty for the edification of Torah knowledge. May the Almighty provide us with the resources we need to establish centers of educational justice for Torah across the Jewish world to enlist all of us to extend the gift of Torah to all of Klal Yisrael. Many have been deprived intentionally or unintentionally from their *mesorah*, and this week's mitzvos teach us to right that wrong.

KI SEITZEI

As our *sidrah* discusses war, it naturally follows to consider what ought to happen with the Jewish soldiers sitting captured at the conclusion of hostilities. The *Rambam* tells us that the greatest mitzvah is redeeming these souls even at great cost, since they stand at great risk with regard to food and to mortal violence while in the hands of vicious enemies. In the Yeshiva in Radin, the Chafetz Chaim would designate students to go out and to share their learning with those at risk spiritually and philosophically. Purportedly, the Rosh Yeshiva would use the following words of returning these individuals to their heritage. The Chafetz Chaim also wrote about equating physical and spiritual well-being (note translation):

> *But alas, today, when because of the yetzer hara, the increase in flagrant depravities everywhere is literally like a raging fire that seeks to destroy all that is good, it is very urgent that groups of G-d-fearing individuals be formed in every community to quench the sheet of fire in their midst.*
>
> *In former times, when fires were infrequent, it was enough for the government to appoint one company of firemen. Today, however, because fires are common everywhere, each community has a group of volunteers...Once it was sufficient for the Holy One, blessed be He, to select a few chosen individuals in each generation who, with the power of their inspired words,*

> *could quench the flame of passion (the holy Alshich in his generation, the Shelah in his generation, the Dubno Maggid in his generation, and others of their caliber), but today, when because of our many sins fires are common everywhere, volunteers must be found in every community.*

Similarly, just like a person might be missing a part of their heritage, which we are then responsible to teach them about, similarly, our *sidrah* teaches us that when a person loses part of his property, his neighbor ought to fulfill the mitzvah of returning it. The Gemara says "*V'hasheivoso lo*" also means an obligation to return himself to himself. In other words, if there's someone in need of being made whole, whether he is cognizant of the loss or not, then we are obligated to help him. So many of our brothers and sisters in and around us, including within our own extended and immediate families, require a deeper sensitivity. It's a legal and ethical failure to not make a call and say, "By the way, you forgot your wallet here, and there's a lot of money inside of it." The same is true regarding a fellow Jew's heritage; through no fault of his own, he may be misinformed about the great value within our Torah tradition.

Lastly, the *Maharal* writes about this week's instruction of caring for the widow and the orphan, that, just like the Almighty looked after us to free us from the depths of Egyptian oppression, so too we must care for those who are often overlooked in our societies. What about those families not in our schools and shuls? And what thought should be given to those who might have been unintentionally ostracized through no fault of their own? Should their children and grandchildren in our midst not be given their right and privilege of taking part in the development of Torah living? Surely, all people of conscience would want to follow the loving ways of the Chafetz Chaim to work towards a Torah-just society. May the Almighty give us the inspiration to always remember that a person's spiritual well-being is our concern just like his financial and physical well-being. And may we instill within our institutions a sense of mission and purpose to always include all of the Almighty's children in our march toward a broader communal *avodas Hashem*!

KI SAVO

In our *sidrah*, we read about the covenant that exists between the entire Jewish People and *Avinu b'Shamayim*. This *bris kodesh* exists innately, which is why Rambam specifies "*kol echad v'echad*," which means each and every Jew when codifying the commandment of loving your fellow. In other words, a special connection exists between Hashem and every Jew, so the same should apply to us. The words in this week's *sidrah* clarify that Am Yisrael is treasured as an *am segulah*, as part of this pact established by our system of mitzvos. The *Netziv* comments that this refers to the added responsibility we have to uphold the 613 obligations that help fortify the world. If a person only looks at his own mitzvah performance, then he is effectually ignoring that everybody in *knesses Yisrael* has this same capacity via his or her connection to the Creator. As Rav Hirsch explains, we see from our *sidrah* that the Jewish People are responsible for representing Torah to the world, which is one of the few benefits of living in the diaspora and having this joint team effort. We read this week that the Torah was written down in stone, and the Mishnah states that it was translated into seventy languages, so that the whole world would be included in its wisdom. Certainly, all the Jews spread around the globe need to have the Torah translated into their respective languages. Language in this context isn't a dialect as much as it is a vocabulary and a way of communicating that fits the times we live in, albeit in a manner that doesn't diminish any authenticity. This effort is part of the greater effort to teach Judaism to Jews. The *pasuk* dictates "*V'halachta b'drachav*," which means to follow in Hashem's ways, *imitatio Dei*, and by specifically being givers and providers. Chazal delineate that this refers to both psychological and substantive giving. Indeed, it's a form of mercy as it states, "*Ma Hu rachum af atah rachum*," which means we are to demonstrate the selflessness of the Almighty as when we were given the Torah in exchange for nothing in return (see *Sefer Hamitzvos* 8 for further discussion of emulation leading toward active benevolence).

In the *tochachah*, we are warned that any wrongdoing will "cling" to us in the collective. All ignorant rebelliousness against the Almighty will lead to separation from the Promised Land. This is stated in the collective and not the singular, as proven by the fact that individuals don't inherit Israel but rather the land is inherited en masse. Unfortunately, one of the punishments that is promised—not so much because of a heavy "hand" as much as a natural consequence—is further illiteracy and obliviousness, as the gap grows between our people and the land. Rabbeinu Tam (1100–1171) describes how only the proliferation of *talmud Torah* can lead to a reversal of this separation from Israel. As the *Netziv* states in the last verse, once individuals learn Torah, then we can nationally know how to live up to our end of the agreement. These are the positive final words of the *sidrah*. The end result is what Hashem gracefully communicates as the crucial objective, which is that the Almighty desires, "*Lemaan taskilu eis kol asher taasun*." May the Almighty assuredly assist us in this endeavor to be successful in all that we do for the sake of Am Yisrael!

NITZAVIM

In our *sidrah*, we recall the national covenant undertaken by Klal Yisrael to uphold the oath sworn to Hakadosh Boruch Hu to be loyal *ovdei Hashem*. We are charged with the opening words, "*Atem nitzavim*," we are standing in acknowledgment. The *Ohr Hachaim* notes that the verse specifies all members of Am Yisrael and then specifies certain subgroups like leaders, children, etc. The commentary notes that, indeed, the *bris* includes those distant and those close to the Almighty. Elders and young are detailed to represent that our collective responsibility is regardless of age. It is also regardless of any other superficial identifier. It is explained that Moshe was striving to drive home the point of *areivus* (mutual responsibility). It is evident from subsequent *pesukim* that the actions of our fellow Jews are our collective obligation. Naturally, the *Ohr Hachaim* states that those who are most informed and most knowledgeable are most accountable. Those in a position to make an impact are expected to do so as part of this final warning by Moshe Rabbeinu. Nobody is exempt from this command, which is why *peshat* according to this *peirush* is the reason for delineating each of the denominations mentioned in the beginning of the *sidrah*.

The Gemara in *Shevuos* reviews the logic behind the words used to administer this national commitment. The specific terms that were ruled out in favor of the words we read this week indicate that this was indeed a timeless promise incumbent upon all Jews to be a part of the broadest adherence possible of the Torah. The Talmud highlights the financial categories as well as all trades, and artisanal representations are emphasized for the effect of total inclusion. Chazal indicate that the covenant was an affirmation and confirmation of Har Sinai to smooth out any possible rationalizations or excuses that could have been made to absolve us from our moral duties in this world. It even goes so far as to cover future generations and future converts who retroactively join in our global commitment, in the sense that they are part of us to the extent that they are considered as having been present at the giving of the Torah. Alas, if haughtiness defines our actions, then our *sidrah* describes that our existence will be overturned with Biblical and Sodom-like destruction. The *sidrah* relates that the nations of the world will describe our existential challenges to be undeniably supernaturally driven via direct punishments from the Almighty. These descriptive warnings are seen as an effort to safeguard us from having alternative influences and influencers inappropriately prioritized before a Torah lifestyle.

Ultimately, we are to envision the most positive of outcomes when the tests and trials run their course and to concede that our fortunes are tied to the Almighty. We read, "*V'shav Hashem Elokecha...v'kibetzcha mi'kol ha'amim*," which means Hashem will return with us as we are gathered from the four corners of the Earth. We are in a permanent relationship, never to be severed. The Almighty isn't married to one Jew alone but rather to each Jew collectively. This is the image Moshe continues with in our *sidrah* to ingrain within us for all time that the idea of mutual responsibility and upholding the everlasting covenant is how we ought to view ourselves. As the *Ohr Hachaim* states, we cannot shrink from this task at hand, and, when we roll up our sleeves to look after our national Torah observance for all of Klal Yisrael, then we will be living up to our end of the *bris kodesh*. Hashem will then take notice of our worthiness of a *hashgachah* that will result in our *geulah sheleimah, kein yehi ratzon.*

VAYEILECH

In our *sidrah*, there is a mitzvah given to us that applies every seven years to every Jew. The *Sefer Hachinuch* refers to it as a pillar of our faith and one of the great honors of our tradition. This is the gathering after *shemittah* for the purposes of hearing the *melech* recite the Torah aloud. It is the greatest of collective learning experiences. The *Kli Yakar* explains that it is to take place on Sukkos because it is the beginning of our calculations for our deeds and misdeeds. During the ten days of awe, the Almighty accepts our supplications for forgiveness and repentance. However, the rest of the year, the power of the *Yamim Noraim* can only be replicated when Klal Yisrael come together en masse. This is the part of the Torah when the *Kli Yakar* describes how the four species bound together on Sukkos are representative of four very different types of Jews. This reinforces that each of us provides atonement for one another. We each lean on the merits of others to fortify our position before the Judge of Judges. In fact, when we are told "*U'lakachtem lachem b'yom ha'rishon*," it doesn't just mean take the *lulav*, *esrog*, *hadasim*, and *aravos* on the first day of the chag; rather it means to take the entirety of Am Yisrael on the first day of our determination to live a mundane life outside of *Aseres Yemei Teshuvah* while striving with the Torah as our guide. The Gemara tells us that the Almighty assesses us as if we were *b'nei maron*, but there are different explanations as to what this means. No matter the definition of *maron*, the Talmud describes how the Almighty scans us as one unit during the judicial process.

The instruction of *Hakhel* is the final message before Hashem tells Moshe that it's time for him to take leave from this world and to prepare the people for the turbulent times that were sure to come following his departure. The fact that we are told that we are going to turn away from Hashem requires us to strategically plan to deal with the foreign influences that threaten our identity. Unfortunately, we are told that after experiencing what appears to be a departure of the Almighty from our midst, we will then describe that the lack of Divine providence proves that Hashem isn't really there at all. These are the times we are living through now. The Torah community is thus obligated to gird our strength to counter the trends of disassociation. We must recall the words of the *Kli Yakar* that our interdependence is unique. By coming together, we possess the power of the awesomeness of Yom Kippur. With that force, we can certainly accomplish a cleansing and a worthiness of a mass *teshuvah* movement. May the Almighty bless us with the strength and the wisdom to raise the level of Klal Yisrael once again so that we can yet experience the *Hakhel* as described in our *sidrah*.

HAAZINU

At the beginning of our *sidrah*, Moshe gives an introduction prior to issuing the famous song capturing the essence of who we are and what our future entails. *Rashi* relays the Gemara's interpretation to us that the source of the practice of reciting *Amen* is found in the third verse of our *sidrah*. Moshe states, "*Ki sheim Hashem ekra*," that as he calls out to the Almighty in blessing, then "*havu godel l'Eilokeinu*," which means the national response of affirmation is going to finalize the *berachah* through their announcement of *Amen*. The institution of *Amen* is more than just a practice; it's a philosophy that we exist as a group that strives to help each other with attaining blessing in our lives. We do not live in a vacuum, and one can't bring glory to Hashem without a national involvement. In other words, a personal exercise that lacks inclusion and interconnectedness pales in comparison to combined efforts.

Remarkably, the context in the aforementioned Gemara (*Berachos* 21a) referenced by *Rashi* is *birkas HaTorah*. Just as Moshe created the mindset and the foundation before this critical *Haazinu* passage, so too before engaging in Torah, one is required to reflect first on the collective intellectual, religious journey upon which he is about to spiritually embark within the context of Hashem's Torah.

V'ZOS HABERACHAH

This week, we recite the famous words, "*Torah tzivah lanu Moshe, morashah kehillas Yaakov*." This verse is arguably one of the most famous lines in the Torah. For generations, young students have been singing the verse of Moshe commanding us the Torah and the inheritance of Yaakov's congregation. We are named Am Yisrael after Yaakov Avinu. The *Netziv* comments that the word "*morashah*" or inheritance specifically implies that the Jewish People obtain this heritage without effort. Understandably, learning and appreciating its contents requires *ameilus* and great academic energy, as Ben Bag Bag states in the fifth chapter of *Avos*, "Turn it over and over...Look deeply into it, grow old with it, spend time over it, do not stir from it..." However, the basic understanding of the great *yerushah* or gift of the Torah is that it belongs to every Jew, even if we do nothing today at all to deserve it.

There is great meaning in labeling our tradition as a birthright given to each and every Jew. The *Netziv* continues that the Jewish People as a whole are given credit for the knowledge of Hashem's Torah spreading throughout the world. It took much more than just the rabbis and scions to allow the ultimate Divine wisdom to flourish within our ranks. We are and have been the collective receptacle for the proliferation of Torah living. The scholars, who are our pillars, could not have succeeded without the broader Jewish People. The *Netziv* explains that this reality provides the depth that the Torah belongs to every Jew, in that like a material inheritance in which no toiling is necessary, so too this intellectual "windfall" is possessed by all Jews regardless of effort. Sometimes, a map to this treasure is all that is needed.

At the end of this *perek*, the practical implications of the resulting worthiness of our people are highlighted with the words "*Ashrecha Yisrael*," meaning we will survive and not follow many other ancient peoples into the abyss of the dustbin of history. In fact, the Aggadata in Tractate *Berachos* tells us that just like Jewish men wear tefillin with parchments praising the Almighty, so too the Almighty wears tefillin with verses inside that praise Klal Yisrael. This description underscores that, as the words herein, "*am nosha*," relate that the endurance of our people is connected to the everlasting endurance of the Almighty's presence perceived in this world. There is a unique, undying character to the individual Jew, even in the World to Come. Rabbeinu Bachya explains our verse and specifically the words of "*ezrecha*" and "*gaava-secha*" as important allusions to instructions to follow the mitzvos. In many respects, Hashem and Klal Yisrael are intertwined. The fate of the stature of Torah and our own fate are intimately connected. The destiny described this week by Moshe rests within our communities. The entire Jewish family must unite to exemplify the bequest from Yaakov Avinu and our ancestors that gets passed down as a *yerushah* from generation to generation.

May the Almighty give us the strength to read each of our *parshiyos* with a keen understanding that inspires us to work toward a plurality of Jews being committed to our mission of representing the Almighty's Torah in this world!

ABOUT THE AUTHOR

Dovid Asher has been the *rav* of Keneseth Beth Israel, the OU synagogue in Central Virginia, since 2011. After ten years in the *beis midrash*, learning in Rabbeinu Yitzchak Elchanan, Aish HaTorah, Mir, Derech HaTalmud, and Shaarei Mevaseret Tziyon, Rabbi Asher continues to teach Torah in a way that encourages a broader sharing of the *chochmas haTorah* with those under-affiliated in the Jewish community. Rabbi Asher is joined in these efforts by his wife, Aliza, and their children, Elana, Yaakov, Ora, and Adir Moshe.